EUROPE BY SLEEPING CAR

MICHAEL PATTERSON

AMBERLEY

The elaborate crest of the Wagons-Lits company was displayed on the exterior of its sleeper, restaurant and Pullman cars. (Tamorlan (File: Logo-Wagons-Lit) [CC BY-SA 3.0] via Wikimedia Commons, 2014*)

First published 2019

Amberley Publishing
The Hill, Stroud,
Gloucestershire, GL5 4EP

www.amberley-books.com

ISBN: 978 1 4456 6924 3 (print)
ISBN: 978 1 4456 6925 0 (ebook)

British Library Cataloguing in Publication Data.
A catalogue record for this book is available from the British Library.

Typeset in 10pt on 13pt Celeste.
Origination by Amberley Publishing.
Printed in the UK.

Introduction

Night trains were once common throughout Europe, but their numbers have dwindled rapidly as low-cost airlines and high-speed rail increasingly offer cheaper and faster ways to travel without having to spend a night on the move. In 1981 there were almost 2,000 sleeping cars in use on hundreds of overnight trains in Continental Europe. For example, sleepers departed every night from the great Paris termini to dozens of destinations as far afield as Copenhagen, Vienna, Naples and Madrid. Today, Paris has only two surviving sleeper services – a nightly train to Venice and a weekly train to Moscow via Berlin and Warsaw – so this book is about a kind of travel experience that has now become something of a rarity.

For me, the sleeping car was a civilised way of making a long European journey – a personal welcome from the attendant, occasionally dinner in the restaurant car, perhaps a nightcap brought to your compartment, drifting off to sleep between crisp white sheets knowing that in the morning you would be somewhere far away, then a wake-up call with a breakfast tray in your cabin. In the 1980s and '90s I made many trips through Europe by train, using sleepers to reach far-flung parts of Italy, Spain and Portugal, Sweden, Norway and Finland. Some of these journeys are at the heart of this book.

For passengers not attracted to the idea of sitting up all night, European night trains offered (and in some cases continue to offer) two options – the sleeping car and the couchette – so it might be helpful to clarify some of the differences. In a couchette there are usually four or six berths per compartment in two tiers of three. Passengers of all genders can find themselves sharing a couchette compartment, so they generally sleep in their daytime clothes, with a sheet, blanket and pillow provided. By contrast, a compartment in a sleeping car normally has one, two or three berths provided with full bedding and is generally allocated exclusively for men or for women unless a couple or family group is travelling together. Unlike couchettes, each sleeper cabin has its own washing facilities and each passenger is provided with soap, a towel and other toiletries. The sleeping car attendant has a separate compartment, often with a small kitchen, and can serve drinks and snacks to passengers in their cabins.

This book is not a history of European sleepers, but it is perhaps worthwhile very briefly to touch on their origins and development. The International Sleeping Car Company (Compagnie Internationale des Wagons-Lits, or just Wagons-Lits for short) was

These beautifully restored vintage vehicles of the Venice–Simplon Orient Express give present-day patrons a taste of the luxury and romance of the golden age of sleeper travel. (Kevin Biétry, 2018)

founded in the 1870s and soon developed a network of long-distance and international trains with sleepers and dining cars across Continental Europe, offering standards of luxury and comfort at a time when train travel was still fairly rough and ready. As well as providing complete trains of carriages, the company supplied individual sleeper or restaurant coaches marshalled in the ordinary trains of state or private railway companies. Until the First World War, Wagons-Lits held a monopoly of international rail travel by sleeper, their operations extending as far as the Trans-Siberian Railway in pre-revolutionary Russia.

In the First World War, much of the company's rolling stock was commandeered for military use. In Germany and Austria-Hungary, Mitropa was founded to take over Wagons-Lits' property and services. In the interwar period the Wagons-Lits company introduced its iconic blue and gold livery, and the fleet reached its maximum of 2,268 vehicles in 1931, marking the zenith of luxury rail travel, with sumptuous interiors created by leading designers and advertising posters that caught the spirit of the age. The Second World War and the post-war division of Europe by the 'Iron Curtain' led to further major disruption of the company's operations.

By 1971 Wagons-Lits had come to realise that the replacement of its ageing and outdated rolling stock was beyond its means. At the end of that year it sold or leased most of its sleeping cars to a pool of nine national railways – Austria, Belgium, Denmark, France, Italy, Luxembourg, the Netherlands, Switzerland and West Germany. An international sleeping

Shorten your long distance trip by a good night's sleep.

Some people prefer to travel during the daytime. Others prefer to travel at night to avoid strain and save time. If you are in the latter category, we recommend a mobile bedroom in a «TEN» sleeping car. They run on almost every main line and are the obvious solution to saving precious business time when travelling to a distant destination.

A map from a publicity leaflet showing the extensive network of Trans Euro Night (TEN) sleeper services operating in the 1980s. Through services are shown to countries such as Spain and Sweden, whose internal sleeper services did not form part of the TEN arrangements. There was limited penetration into Central and Eastern Europe, which was then still separated from the West by the 'Iron Curtain'. (Author's collection)

car pool named TEN (Trans Euro Night) was founded, which took over and managed many of the carriages of the Wagons-Lits company, as well as those of Mitropa's successor in West Germany, Deutsche Schlafwagen Gesellschaft (DSG). However, Wagons-Lits and DSG continued to provide the staffing, catering, servicing and bed linen for all sleeping cars operated by the TEN pool – an arrangement that lasted until 1995.

Throughout their history, Continental sleeper trains came to acquire an aura of intrigue and romance, and some developed a rather risqué reputation with tales of ladies of the night; a former chairman of the BBC is even rumoured to have submitted an expenses claim for hiring a prostitute on the Orient Express. While I personally encountered nothing that might have brought a blush to the cheeks of a maiden aunt on my own journeys, I hope this book nevertheless captures something of the glamour and uniqueness of sleeper travel.

Layouts of sleeping car types used on journeys in this book

Type F (built 1936-52) Night Ferry

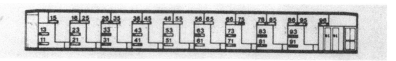

T2 (1968-72) Napoli Express, Palatino, La Palombe Bleue, Nord Express

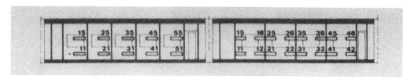

TcA, TcB (1974 and 1981) Barcelona Talgo, Paris-Madrid Talgo

YF (1963-72) Spain and Portugal

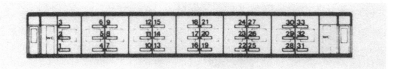

WL/SJ (1946-65) Sweden

AB33 (1959-73) Frankfurt-Copenhagen

To Italy

Night Ferry

For me, a book about European sleeper trains has to begin with the Night Ferry. It was a truly remarkable train – Britain's only scheduled through passenger service to and from the Continent before the opening of the Channel Tunnel in 1994. From 1936 until 1980, except during the Second World War and its aftermath, it ran nightly from London's Victoria station, initially to Paris and also to Brussels from 1957. Contrary to popular myth, passengers using the Golden Arrow had to leave their Pullman cars at the Channel port, transfer to the ship, and join a different set of Pullman cars at the French port for their onward journey to Paris. Passengers on the Night Ferry had no such inconvenience; they joined the train at London Victoria in mid-evening and disembarked in Lille, Paris or Brussels the next morning, the sleeping cars having been shunted onto a train-ferry at Dover and off again at Dunkirk in France.

In the autumn of 1969, as part of my university course I was sent to a school at Douai in northern France to spend an academic year as an English assistant. I travelled from London to Lille by the Night Ferry, although I went down to Dover in an ordinary seating carriage attached to the sleeping cars, made my way onto the ferry, sat in the ship's bar, and completed my journey the next morning after a sleepless night. I arrived somewhat the worse for wear for my interview with the school's principal and, after dinner with the vice-principal and his family that night, finally collapsed into bed in my hastily arranged lodgings, having been awake for the best part of forty-eight hours.

The Paris to London section of the Night Ferry was routed through Douai, although the train did not stop there. From my room in the late evening, I could hear it approaching before the sound of its progress was briefly muffled by the town. Thirty seconds or so later it would burst out into the countryside again as it continued towards Lille, the distinctive rhythm of the baggage vans on the jointed track giving the train a unique sound profile. Homesick at first, I longed to be on board, and when I returned to England for Christmas

The Italian journey, with the route taken shown in red.

For many years these illuminated signs – 'The Night Ferry' and 'Paris, Brussels' – were displayed above Platforms 1 and 2 at London Victoria station. They are now on display at the National Railway Museum in York. (Reinhard Dietrich (Own work) [Public Domain] via Wikimedia Commons, 2009*)

Double-headed, the Night Ferry approaches London during the last days of steam on the Kent main lines. (Robert Carroll, *c.* 1959)

A Class 71 electric loco in sole charge of the Night Ferry as it nears London on the last leg of its journey. (Robert Carroll, 1967)

This remarkable photograph taken near Petts Wood captures the inbound Night Ferry (left), running very late as it passes the outbound Golden Arrow, which is heading for Dover (right). This may be the only photograph in existence of the two trains together. (Robert Carroll, 1968)

I made it my business to book a sleeper berth. On joining the train at Lille I found myself sharing a compartment with a chatty Irishman who had a bad cold, had drunk one too many nightcaps and was none too fragrant. I did manage to get some sleep but made a mental note always to reserve a compartment for myself whenever I travelled by sleeper again.

The sleeping cars for the Night Ferry were a special type (named 'F' for Ferry). They were shorter than standard European sleepers and had sides that tapered towards the roof. This allowed them to operate on the Southern Railway with its tight loading gauge and narrow tunnels. Each sleeper had eighteen berths in nine compartments, which could be used as singles or doubles. Initially passengers sharing a compartment needed only second-class tickets, but from 1956 the sleepers became first class only and a passenger wanting a compartment for sole use had to pay extra.

Twelve sleepers were built for the initial service in 1936 and six more were added when the train started running again in 1947, partly to replace vehicles lost or destroyed during the Second World War. A further seven cars were brought into service in 1952. Each train normally consisted of six sleepers, but up to nine were used at busy times. Initially restaurant cars served dinner and breakfast on both sides of the Channel, although the northbound train from Paris lost its diner after being re-routed via Lille in 1966. With English passengers in mind, a cooked breakfast was even available between Dunkirk and Paris on the southbound journey. For the ferry crossing, the train was split into sections to ensure that the weight was evenly distributed on board the ship. Life jackets were provided in each compartment. A locked dock and linkspan had to be constructed at Dover to enable the water level to be raised or lowered so that the rails on the ship were level with those on the landward side. From 1967 until 1969, a London-Basel car was added to the train, but it was not a success.

In 1977 French Railways (SNCF) bought or leased the sleeping cars from Wagons-Lits, and British Rail staff took over the duties of the on-board attendants. The sleepers lost their distinctive Wagons-Lits crests and some were repainted in SNCF livery. The restaurant cars were replaced by a buffet or trolley service. Attempts were made to refresh the train's image, but patronage was already in decline and replacing the forty-year-old sleepers was out of the question. At that time I lived in Kent. Waiting at the local station on my morning commute, I would occasionally see the London-bound Night Ferry sweep through, causing confusion for unwary commuters for whom this exotic foreign train seemed a complete mystery.

I had a last chance to use the Night Ferry during its final week of operation before withdrawal on 31 October 1980. Although I was on my way to Italy, the Paris cars were fully booked, so I had no option but to travel in one of the Brussels cars, which was not the most obvious route. As usual, the train left from Platform 2 at London Victoria, which was sealed off because customs checks were carried out before passengers boarded. This time I took no chances and booked a compartment for my exclusive use. My carriage seemed to be full of boisterous passengers trying out this unique service for the first and last time. The people in the next compartment spent quite some time trying to break through the connecting door into mine, apparently under the illusion that a sleeper cabin was like Doctor Who's TARDIS – much bigger inside than it looks on the outside.

In truth, travelling on the Night Ferry was never a particularly restful experience. The journey to Dover took less than an hour and a half, and on arrival there was much jolting as the train was divided and shunted onto the ferry. There it was fixed to the deck with heavy chains by men whose job apparently required them to shout instructions to each other without much regard for passengers trying to sleep. There followed a constant procession of people leaving the sleepers to buy their duty-free on board the ship before returning to noisily show off their purchases to their travelling companions. At Dunkirk, the chains were removed and there was further shunting as the Brussels and Paris coaches were re-marshalled into two separate trains for the final parts of their respective journeys. What seemed on paper a romantic journey to the Continent in pre-war sleeping cars was in reality a recipe for a fitful night's rest.

The Night Ferry could not have survived the opening of the Channel Tunnel and its associated high-speed lines. Paris and Brussels are now little more than two hours from London. However, detailed plans were published for the introduction of NightStar sleeper services through the Channel Tunnel from London to Amsterdam, Dortmund and Frankfurt, and from Paris to Plymouth, Swansea, Manchester and Glasgow, starting in 1996. A special fleet of 139 vehicles, including seventy-two sleepers, forty-seven seating coaches and twenty lounge cars, was built. Each sleeper had ten two-berth cabins – each with a toilet – and some were equipped with showers. Test runs of the new trains took place in 1997 but timescales had already slipped. When it became clear that traffic levels on daytime Eurostar services were well below expectations, the NightStars were put on hold. The project was formally cancelled in 1999 and all 139 vehicles were later sold to Canadian operator VIA Rail. Given that the trains had already been built, it seems a great pity that NightStar was not at least given a chance to prove itself. The fate of most other European sleeper services since the 1990s suggests that it would have been an uphill struggle, but I can't help but wonder what might have been.

Napoli Express

Having said a last goodbye to the Night Ferry in Brussels, all I had to do now was to reach Paris in time for my next sleeper, which would take me to Italy. Paris was then undoubtedly the most important hub for sleeper services in Western Europe. From the Gare d'Austerlitz, Est, Lyon or Nord, sleeping cars departed for most major cities on the European mainland, as well as to many of the great cities of France. Space does not permit a complete list, but in 1980 passengers could travel to London, Hamburg, Copenhagen, Berlin, Warsaw, Moscow, Zurich, Munich, Vienna, Bucharest, Milan, Rome, Naples, Venice, Barcelona or Madrid by direct sleeper from Paris. While London was about to be deleted from that list, and the three-night journey to Istanbul on the Orient Express had already ceased in 1977, the sleeping car network was still extensive and apparently flourishing.

In reality the economics of sleeper services were already in trouble but their gradual demise was going to be a slow process. Well into the 1990s it was still possible to spend a fascinating evening at the Gare de Lyon in Paris watching night trains depart for Rome, Venice, Florence, Genoa and Milan, each with its complement of up to four gleaming blue

The sleeping cars of the Night Ferry await their passengers at Victoria station. (Roger Sutcliffe, 1979)

The stock of the last ever Night Ferry is shunted into Victoria carriage sidings after the train's final run. The sleeping car is in SNCF livery. (John Law, 1980)

What might have been – NightStar carriages built for use on Channel Tunnel sleeper services, which were never introduced. (Alisdair Anderson, 2000)

The Napoli Express approaching Paris at the end of its nineteen-hour journey from southern Italy. The blue TEN sleeping car is immediately behind the loco. (Michel Ledieu, 1990)

sleeping cars, followed by domestic sleeper services to a range of destinations including Nice, Béziers, Briançon, Moutiers, Bourg St Maurice and Saint-Gervais.

One evening after dinner I wandered across to the station to watch proceedings. Wearing a suit and tie underneath my old railway supervisor's overcoat, which kept out the bitter cold of the February night, perhaps it should have occurred to me that I might be mistaken for an official of the SNCF as I strolled up and down the platforms observing proceedings, and I was in fact approached several times by both passengers and train crew for information. Platforms were thronged with passengers and people who had come to see them off, while trains were packed and the Gare de Lyon was operating flat out. For me as a railwayman, it was an exhilarating experience to watch as the shrill urgency of the supervisor's whistle encouraged latecomers to get on board before each train of up to sixteen carriages began to move, imperceptibly at first, before gliding out of the station into the night.

My berth on the Napoli Express from the Gare de Lyon to Turin was in a modern sleeper, shiny and gleaming in contrast to the very tired pre-war carriage of the previous night's journey on the Night Ferry. These T2-type sleepers, of which 188 were built between 1968 and 1980, had a layout cleverly arranged on two levels to provide thirty-six berths in eighteen cabins. The lower compartments could be used as small first-class singles (known as specials) or as two-berth second-class doubles. The upper compartments had two berths on either side of the floor space for use by travellers with second-class tickets. My bed was already made up in time for departure at 20.39, so, having handed over my tickets, reservations and passport to the sleeping car conductor sitting at the end of the corridor, from where he could keep an eye on all his charges, I grabbed the opportunity to get an early night. This time the ride was gratifyingly smooth and quiet and I slept soundly as the Napoli Express sped south-east across France.

I was asleep when the train arrived at Chambéry in the French Alps at just after two in the morning. There, the Turin sleeper was detached from the main train and the Napoli Express continued on its way to southern Italy, where it would arrive in Naples sometime after five in the afternoon. After more than an hour at Chambéry, my sleeper was attached to another train to complete its journey, eventually depositing its passengers in Turin at the civilised hour of 07.30, long after the main Napoli Express had made its call there in the early hours. The introduction of high-speed TGV services between Paris and Milan in 1996 revolutionised transit times between Paris and Italy, and spelled the end for the Napoli Express and its twenty-hour journey time. Passengers for Naples still had the option of taking the Paris–Rome sleeper and continuing by day train, but the separate Paris–Turin sleeping car had long since disappeared by that time.

After the wet and gloomy weather of Belgium and France, the magnificent vista of snow-capped mountains set against a clear blue Italian sky lifted the spirits as the train descended from the Alps. Turin's Porta Nuova station is built on a monumental scale, the passenger facilities being located in a series of vast marble halls. In the booking hall it was not so much a matter of queuing to buy a ticket as pushing to the front of a jostling crowd at one of several ticket windows. Outside, the bright morning sun lit up the station's great edifice while, in the shade of a long colonnade, members of the shoeshine team were setting up for the day's work.

By Train Around Italy's Coastline

Hours spent poring over Thomas Cook's International Timetable when planning this trip had revealed that it was possible to travel by train around the entire coastline of Italy, from Genoa in the west to Reggio di Calabria on the 'toe', across to Brindisi on the 'heel', and finally returning north along the Adriatic coast. It was a memorable journey: a spectacular sunset over the island of Elba where Napoleon Bonaparte was briefly exiled; the charming ritual of *la passeggiata*, whole families strolling arm-in-arm in their Sunday best along the main street, stopping from time to time to greet friends and neighbours; Mount Vesuvius, the volcano looming over Naples, which destroyed the ancient city of Pompeii; and lunch in the restaurant car of a crack express called Aurora as it sped south from Naples along the coastline of the Tyrrhenian Sea. Stepping off this air-conditioned train at Reggio di Calabria in Italy's deep south was like opening the door of a hot oven.

Much of Italy is mountainous and its landscape spectacular, with countless villages and old towns set high on the hillsides. The journey between Reggio and Taranto was different: wild and remote with unspoilt deserted beaches along the coast of the Ionian Sea. At one station an old lady dressed in black joined me in my compartment in what was otherwise an almost empty carriage and, having placed her shopping on the next seat, began chatting away despite my inability to understand a word. I tried to explain that I did not speak Italian, but it didn't matter; she wanted some company for her short journey. A couple of stops later, I helped her descend the steep steps to the low platform and handed down her shopping bags.

As the line followed the twists and turns of the coastline, progress was at a gentle pace. In fact, the schedule seemed likely to have been much the same as in the days of steam. I reached the Adriatic coast at Brindisi, where a 2,000-year-old column marks the end of the Appian Way, the ancient road to Rome. The next day, the railways were on strike. In Italy that meant a limited service had to be provided, but with trains liable to suffering severe delay. The express I was due to catch did run, but became increasingly late as the day wore on, until it was eventually an hour and a half behind schedule. As dusk fell, I bailed out at the seaside resort of Termoli, to be greeted by dark clouds and heavy rain, as if confirming the onset of autumn.

On my last day in Italy I had to recoup the time lost during the previous day's 'strike' by making an early start. This meant a ten-hour journey on just one train, for most of the way travelling along the beautiful Adriatic coast. I was just beginning to enjoy the ride when a young couple joined the train and sat in my otherwise empty compartment. Sitting opposite each other they began a loud and lengthy argument, as if they had failed to notice that they were sharing the compartment with a complete stranger. My patience finally snapped when they both lit up, and I pointed out in my best broken Italian that it was a non-smoking compartment. They appeared astonished at this intervention as no-smoking signs in Italy seemed to be regarded as a health warning rather than an instruction, but they departed without further ado. My embarrassment at having caused them to leave lasted no longer than the remaining cigarette smoke took to clear.

A T2 sleeper. This type of coach has small single compartments called Specials for passengers travelling in first class (the larger windows in this photograph) and small double compartments in second class (the upper windows). (Author, 1992)

The snow-covered Alps form a spectacular backdrop as the railway descends from the French–Italian border towards Turin. (Paolo Taesi, 2018)

The vast marble halls of Turin's Porta Nuova station. (Author, 1980)

Mount Vesuvius, as seen from Naples. (Wolfgang Moroder (Own work) [CC BY-SA 3.0] via Wikimedia Commons, 2017*)

Palatino

My Italian journey ended in Modena, a prosperous city that seemed full of elegant people who looked as if they were in a fashion shoot as they made their evening *passeggiata*. From here I was booked on an overnight express called Palatino for the twelve-hour journey back to Paris. As the gleaming sleeping cars came to a halt, the door of my carriage opened and the smartly uniformed conductor stepped onto the platform to greet me and show me to my cabin; I was expected, which is always something of a relief when you are travelling by sleeper. The train was formed of two sections which came together at Turin. It was the section that started from Florence that picked me up at Modena, while the coaches from Rome travelled via Genoa.

Palatino started life in 1890 as the Rome Express, a service run by Wagons-Lits that was interrupted only during the Second World War. A British feature film called *Rome Express* was released in 1932. Like many movies set on trains, it was a thriller involving murder and a shady cast of characters. The real train originally had through sleepers to Calais for connections by ship to England, but these ended in 1969, when the train's name was changed to Palatino. The Paris–Rome sleeper service eventually suffered a stuttering demise. In 2011 it was discontinued after a new company took over operation of the Paris–Italy night services. It was revived in 2012 but ceased operation once again at the end of 2013, this time permanently, leaving the service to Venice as the last surviving nightly sleeper train between Paris and Italy. Travellers from Paris to Rome can now make the journey by day train, changing at Turin or Milan, but it is still possible to travel overnight by taking an afternoon TGV from Paris to Turin, from where sleeper trains still run to Rome and Naples.

Before arriving in Paris I enjoyed a tray breakfast brought to my cabin, declining the offer of something more substantial in the Gril-Express car, which had been attached to the train at Chambéry. The last day of my tour was taken up with a classic journey from Paris to London by boat train and ship. In those far-off days before the opening of the Channel Tunnel, the journey from Paris to London took nearly seven hours, compared with little more than two by Eurostar today – a prime example of how high-speed lines have revolutionised rail travel in Europe. My Italian odyssey ended, as it had begun, at London's Victoria station. The only difference was that the train on which I had started my journey ten days earlier, the Night Ferry, had now passed into history.

The railway runs past endless unspoilt beaches on the Ionian coast between Reggio di Calabria and Taranto. (Fabio Miotto, 2017)

Brindisi by night – the terminal column of the Appian Way, the ancient road to Rome. (Livioandronico2013 (Own work) [CC BY-SA 3.0] via Wikimedia Commons, 2015*)

In later years, the Paris–Italy night trains were re-routed to run via Switzerland. Here, the southbound Palatino calls at Lausanne. (NAC [CC BY-SA 4.0] via Wikimedia Commons, 2010*)

The Paris–Venice sleeper is now the sole survivor of numerous Paris–Italy overnight services. The train is seen here near Brescia, in northern Italy. (Paolo Taesi, 2013)

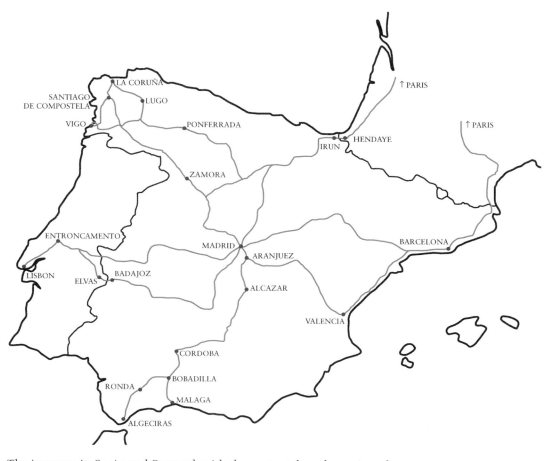

The journeys in Spain and Portugal, with the routes taken shown in red.

To Northern Spain

London to Paris via Harwich and the Hook of Holland

I suspect comparatively few journeys from London to Spain have begun with dinner in the restaurant car of the 6.10 p.m. train from Liverpool Street to Norwich. In 1982 I was heading for Coruña in the far north-west of Spain and had decided to gain an extra day's travelling by setting out on Friday night rather than Saturday morning. With the Night Ferry now just a fond memory, the only realistic alternative offering the prospect of a decent night's rest en route to the Continent was the overnight sailing from Harwich to the Hook of Holland.

So here I was, scoffing a three-course dinner in the sixty-six minutes the train took to travel from Liverpool Street to Manningtree in Essex, where I had to change for the local service to Harwich Parkeston Quay.

I could, of course, have enjoyed the relaxing atmosphere of the ship's restaurant rather than risking indigestion from bolting down a British Rail dinner, but the shipping forecast was not good and I am a poor sailor. I aimed to eat early and be in bed before the ship set off into a stormy North Sea. Safely tucked up in my cabin, I hardly noticed what turned out to be quite a rough night, and was even in the mood for a hearty breakfast the next morning, while many of my fellow passengers were still looking decidedly green about the gills.

The Hook of Holland was once the starting point for a range of Continental night trains. Passengers from England could connect into these out of the daytime sailing from Harwich. For example, in 1972 sleeper services left the Hook for Copenhagen, Moscow and various places in Austria. None survive today.

From the Hook, a short train ride delivered me to Rotterdam Central station. The clean lines of this striking modern building and its vast booking hall were impressive. Built between 1950 and 1957, the wide curving glass frontage and the interior finishes created a sense of space and efficiency. It may seem fanciful, but the sight of many well-dressed and prosperous-looking passengers forming orderly queues at the long line of ticket windows somehow put me in mind of the railway station and airport scenes in Alfred Hitchcock's thriller *North by North West*. It was like a bustling recreation of late 1950s New York, albeit without the drama. Sadly, this beautiful station building proved unable to cope with increasing passenger numbers and was replaced in 2008. From Rotterdam I took a

The Hook of Holland. The green carriage is a Soviet Union (USSR) sleeping car. Before the Iron Curtain and the Berlin Wall came down in 1989, USSR sleeper services linked Moscow to most Western European capitals, as well as to Ostend and the Hook for onward travel to London by rail and ship. The sleeper from the Hook to Moscow ran four times a week and took two nights to complete the journey. (Cornelius Koelewijn, 1988)

The busy booking hall of Rotterdam Central station, reminiscent of a scene from *North by Northwest*. (Author, 1982)

round-about route to Paris via Amsterdam, Maastricht and Liège, where tight connections of just a few minutes all worked perfectly. They needed to; otherwise, I might well have missed my sleeper to Barcelona. In those days, I still had a touching faith in the punctuality and efficiency of European railways.

Barcelona Talgo

From the Gare du Nord in Paris I crossed to Austerlitz station for the Barcelona Talgo, a train of small articulated air-conditioned sleeping cars. The first-class coaches had five compartments for use as singles or doubles, while the second-class coaches had four compartments with four berths in each. First introduced in 1974, the trains were specially designed to operate in both France and Spain, the coaches being jacked up at the border to adjust the wheelsets from European standard gauge to Spanish broad gauge without disturbing the sleeping passengers on board. Before 1974 passengers from Paris would catch the Barcelona Express and change trains at the Spanish border. When it was first introduced in 1903 by Wagons-Lits, the Barcelona Express connected to a Pullman train to complete the journey.

At first sight the Barcelona Talgo had something of the appearance of a London Tube train, its short squat coaches sitting low down on the track. This lowered the train's centre of gravity, allowing higher speeds and providing greater stability on the curving broad gauge tracks of Spain's main lines. In addition to the sleeping cars, a restaurant car served dinner upon leaving Paris at 9 p.m. I decided to eat before boarding to avoid trying to sleep on a full stomach. I had yet to learn that people eat their evening meal late in Spain.

I had visited Barcelona once before, when Spain was still a dictatorship under General Franco. The city had been a centre of opposition to Franco during the Spanish Civil War in the 1930s and had continued to pay a heavy price for backing the losing side. In 1974, Barcelona had struck me as a rundown and depressing place. At my hotel, near the station, I was shown to a room that was one of many leading directly off a large dancefloor. The odours emanating from the bathroom plumbing were less than fragrant and my exploration of the city included a search for disinfectant and bleach. Returning to my room after dinner, I found a dance in full swing and threaded my way between smooching couples, some of whom disappeared into the other bedrooms leading off the dance floor. It began to dawn on me what sort of establishment this might be. I retreated to my room and made sure the door was firmly locked, slightly surprised that my bed was not already occupied.

The Talgo's twelve-hour journey from Paris ended at Barcelona's Termino station. Termino was one of the city's principal stations, but today most long-distance services are concentrated on the rebuilt Sants station, and Termino has been renamed França. By 1982 Spain had become a democracy, but I did begin to wonder whether the spirit of Franco lived on. Passengers from the Talgo were made to line up on the platform and then marched across the concourse behind a uniformed officer of military bearing for a customs inspection. The Barcelona Talgo was renamed Juán Miró in 1992. The original Talgo trainset was then replaced by a Trenhotel (hotel train), some of whose compartments were equipped with separate shower and toilet facilities. This service ended in 2013 when the new high-speed line from Perpignan in France to Barcelona opened, allowing through day trains from Paris to complete the journey to Barcelona in under seven hours.

My onward train to Madrid was scheduled to take nearly nine hours. This was long before the high-speed AVE line between the two cities reduced journey times to just two and a half hours. In fact, my journey took a good deal longer than nine hours and put the connection with my next sleeper in jeopardy. It was a spectacular ride, though, with long sections through completely barren landscapes or in the shadow of high sierras. At one point, a main-line steam locomotive stood abandoned on a siding in the middle of nowhere, apparently just left there when its time in service had run out. Lunch was served to first-class passengers at their seat on a tray plugged into a slot in the armrests. There was a set menu, which, to my astonishment, consisted of no less than five courses. With half a bottle of wine and a coffee afterwards, the entire bill came to less than £5. It was my first introduction to the high standards and value for money of Spanish train meals.

Rías Altas

I had planned to have two hours to transfer from Madrid Chamartin to Norte (Principe Pío) station to catch my next sleeper to La Coruña, but the train from Barcelona was so late that it was all a bit of a rush. On arrival at Norte I found myself manhandling my luggage down a narrow iron staircase, which seemed to descend from the roof of a vast barn of a station in which several overnight trains were already boarding. I was clearly in such a hurry that I had missed the main entrance. My compartment was in gleaming blue sleeping car No. 4654, dating from the 1960s. The train, named Rías Altas – a reference to the northern coastal estuaries of Galicia – departed at 21.25. Although there was a restaurant car, I was still groaning after my heavy lunch so gave dinner a miss, especially at that late hour.

In the morning I awoke just as dawn was breaking over the cathedral city of Santiago de Compostela. It was almost nine o'clock and the smell of coal smoke was drifting into my compartment, which made me wonder whether the train had a steam locomotive. It didn't, but an equally interesting explanation was revealed when I went for breakfast. The restaurant car was a real antique – built in 1928 according to the manufacturer's plates. Most of the coach was taken up by the seating area, at one end of which was a bar. Behind the bar was the kitchen area and, beyond that, a small coal-fired boiler room, complete with sacks of coal and long metal shovels. This was the source of the coal smoke I had smelled earlier.

The train acquired the name Rías Altas in about 1975. Around the millennium it was renamed Rías Gallegas (Galician Estuaries), but the opening of new sections of the Madrid–Galicia high-speed line from 2011 onwards brought an end to the direct sleeper service via Santiago. Nevertheless, it is still possible to make the overnight journey from Madrid to La Coruña by taking the hotel train Atlántico, which is routed via León.

Lugo and Ponferrada

My arrival at La Coruña was over an hour late. The journey onwards to Lugo revealed a very different landscape from the barren wildernesses of the previous day. Here in Galicia, Spain's most north-westerly province, the landscape is lush and green, well-watered by rains blowing in off the Atlantic.

The Barcelona Talgo at Paris-Austerlitz. (Torrego family, 1986)

Old- and new-style Talgo trains under the curving roof of Barcelona Termino. (Jorge Almuni Ruiz, 2014)

Night trains at Madrid's Principe Pío station. (Ramiro C., 1986, courtesy of the Torrego family)

Restaurant car No. 3567, similar to the one that provided dinner and breakfast on my journey from Madrid to La Coruña in 1982. Now preserved and restored to its former glory, the carriage's coal-fired boiler is still visibly in working order. (Jorge Almuni Ruiz, 2009)

An early afternoon arrival in Lugo gave me plenty of time to look around, but first I had to find somewhere to stay. After three nights on the move, I was pretty tired, so when I came across a substantial building displaying a neon sign announcing that it was a two-star hostal, I lazily assumed that this might be an alternative Spanish word for hotel, rather than what it turned out to be – a second-rate guest house. I realised my mistake too late. From the depths of her armchair, a toothless old woman in carpet slippers assessed my suitability as a guest before agreeing to rent me a room. She spoke loudly and slowly in Spanish so I could understand. I couldn't. My one night's stay plus breakfast cost 535 pesetas (about £2.95). As I didn't have a banknote small enough, I had to go out for some change. Lugo itself is an interesting place, however. Its ancient walls afford spectacular views of the surrounding countryside and some fascinating glimpses of the city's cathedral and quaint old houses.

Next morning was clear and bright as I set out on the relatively short journey to Ponferrada. The train was a long-distance diesel unit consisting of just two coaches – one first class, one second. While there was something of a scramble for seats in second class, I found myself sitting in splendid isolation in the first-class carriage. Not only that, but this train offered a hot meal service, which, once again, was provided on a tray plugged into the armrests of my seat. The menu was limited but a freshly cooked tortilla was just what I needed for lunch after a rather sparse breakfast.

Ponferrada is a much more interesting place than I had assumed. The star attraction is undoubtedly the castle, which was built for the Knights Templar in around 1300. It sits on a bluff above the town and its ancient stone walls glow golden in the sunlight. At the time of my visit, much of the old town struck me as being in worse condition than it would have been centuries earlier at the height of Spain's power. Conservation and urban renewal seemed noticeably lacking and many fine medieval buildings had been allowed to deteriorate into little more than slums. One other attraction, for me at least, was that Ponferrada was the terminus of a narrow-gauge mineral railway, and in the yard a steam engine was marshalling coal wagons. Despite the existence of a station, there was no sign of any passenger trains or any information to suggest that a service still operated on the line to Villablino. In fact, the passenger service was abandoned two years before my visit.

Zamora, Santiago de Compostela and Vigo

I made another trip to northern Spain in 1985, this time with Santiago de Compostela as my principal destination. On the way I stopped off in Zamora, a city with an exceptional number of beautiful twelfth- and thirteenth-century Romanesque churches. Tired and footsore after visiting so many of them, I went in search of a drink on what was a warm evening and found myself in a busy bar, where I ordered a gin and tonic in halting Spanish like a cartoon Englishman. This was clearly an unusual order in these un-touristy parts, but, undaunted, the barman produced a litre bottle of Gordon's and proceeded to half-fill a very large glass, to which he added a splash of tonic from a small bottle. Even with the whole bottle of tonic added, this proved to be just about the stiffest G&T I ever had the pleasure of drinking, and at a fraction of the price normally charged in an English bar for the usual miserable measure of gin. I slept like a log.

As luck would have it, I arrived in Santiago on Mardi Gras. To celebrate the last day before the sacrifices of Lent, the inhabitants organise a huge procession from the cathedral square through the streets of the city, with many people dressed up in masks and costumes. Here was 'Prince Charles'; there a group of '*falangists*', who risked annoying the crowds with their mock salutes, although the good-humoured nature of the event was not threatened. Santiago is one of the great pilgrimage centres of Europe, having a silver casket in its vast cathedral containing the remains of Christ's Apostle, Saint James. The entrance to the cathedral is through the magnificent Portico de la Gloria, carved in exquisite detail between 1168 and 1188. The cathedral also boasts the largest censer in the world, which on special occasions is swung enthusiastically from the rafters on a very long rope, with clouds of incense pouring out as it swings to and fro in the most alarming way over worshippers' heads.

After dinner I sauntered down to the station to watch the departure of the overnight sleeper from La Coruña to Madrid. To my amazement the restaurant car was an antique vehicle similar to the one I came across in 1982. It was coach number 3567 and its manufacturer's plate bore the date 1930. This carriage had been in service for no less than fifty-five years, providing meals and refreshments to passengers on Spain's railways since before the Spanish Civil War. To a railwayman such as myself, here was a direct link to a past every bit as poignant as the twelfth-century carvings on the Portico de la Gloria.

The following morning I had time to attend an Ash Wednesday Mass in the cathedral before making the two-hour journey through typical Galician countryside and along the coast to the port city of Vigo. A climb up to the castle and its gardens was rewarded with spectacular views to the mouth of the estuary and beyond. In the evening the view from my hotel window was dominated by the harbour lights. It called to mind a scene in the German war movie *Das Boot* (The Boat), where a U-boat surfaces on a dead calm night inside Vigo harbour. Aching for the safety and comforts of a home port, but desperate to avoid detection in the waters of neutral Spain, the crew members gaze longingly at the lights of the city while they rendezvous with an impounded German vessel, from which they are to obtain fresh supplies.

La Palombe Bleue

Both my trips to northern Spain concluded with long journeys back to the French border, the magnificent countryside unfolding for hour after hour. On the International Bridge between Irun, the last station in Spain, and Hendaye, the first in France, the railway tracks are arranged so that trains of both standard and broad gauge can use them. My overnight train to Paris was called La Palombe Bleue (Blue Dove) and my compartment was in one of the familiar T2-type sleeping cars. As always with this type of sleeper, the ride was smooth and quiet – sometimes to the point where it was difficult to know if the train was actually moving. At Dax, the train joined up with sleepers from Tarbes and Lourdes for the journey to Paris.

La Palombe Bleue began life as the Pyrénées–Côte d'Argent Express in 1889, one of the Wagons-Lits company's deluxe trains. Like La Palombe Bleue, it had portions from Hendaye and Tarbes to Paris. The purpose of the Hendaye portion was in part to make a connection with trains from the Spanish railway network, which had reached the French

A view of Lugo, in Galicia, from the city's Roman walls. (Pascal Poggi, 2014)

A long-distance regional unit of the type used on my daytime journeys in northern Spain: one first-class coach (yellow stripe above the windows), one second-class. (Luis Ignacio Alonso, 1987)

Ponferrada – the twelfth-century castle of the Knights Templar. (Author, 1982)

LRF 250 Madrid-Chamartín - Pontevedra

A Madrid–Pontevedra train passes over the spectacular Martin Gil Viaduct near Zamora. (Jesús M. Velasco, 2017)

The cathedral of Santiago de Compostela, one of the great pilgrimage centres of Europe. (Pascal Poggi, 2011)

Restaurant car No. 3567, built in 1930. This car was still in regular service in 1985, when I came across it at Santiago on an overnight train from La Coruña to Madrid. (Jorge Almuni Ruiz, 2009)

border in 1887. Later, the sleepers from Hendaye to Paris formed part of the Iberia Express, which included couchettes from Madrid and Algeciras whose wheelsets had to be changed at the border on account of the difference in track gauge. The name Palombe Bleue was introduced in the late 1970s. The train lost its sleeping cars in the early 2000s, but continued to operate with couchettes until June 2017, when, despite protests, it was finally withdrawn on the completion of the Paris–Bordeaux high-speed line.

Over the years I used La Palombe Bleue several times when returning from Spain. On one occasion the sleeping car conductor warned me to make sure my compartment door was locked when I went to bed and not to open it if someone knocked. I don't know what prompted this advice but, sure enough, somewhere along the line quite a crowd joined the train and someone knocked on the door of my compartment and tried to get in. The conductor was soon on the scene to move the potential intruder on. I never discovered whether this was a genuine sleeper passenger in the wrong coach or someone chancing his luck.

Arrival at Paris-Austerlitz was at 07.15, after which I took the Metro to St Lazare station for the journey home to London via Dieppe and Newhaven. For many years the Metro had become increasingly decrepit and in 1975 I had written on a postcard home: 'One of these days the Metro will fall to pieces.' Since then, there had been a marked modernisation of the system, so I was amazed in 1982 to find myself travelling on a Metro train dating back to the time of the First World War. It was in fact the last full year of operation for these Sprague-Thomson units on Line 9 before the withdrawal of the ancient red (first class) and green (second class) carriages that had for so long given the Paris Metro its unique character. I reached St Lazare station in the middle of the morning rush hour – an impressive sight, with commuters thronging every passageway, staircase and escalator – and then travelled on to Dieppe, with a pleasant crossing to Newhaven spent largely in the ship's restaurant, enjoying a good lunch, and then home.

The port city of Vigo on Spain's Atlantic coast. (Thorcho gp [CC BY-SA 3.0] via Wikimedia Commons, 2013*)

A preserved Sprague-Thomson unit with first- and second-class carriages. Introduced in the early years of the twentieth century, these units helped give the Paris Metro its unique character. Despite massive modernisation of the Metro system in the 1970s, some of these units remained in regular service, and I found myself travelling on one when returning from northern Spain in 1982, shortly before they were finally phased out. (Dominique Desmares, 2001)

To Andalusia

Calais

Before Spain built its high-speed AVE network, journeys that can now be done in a couple of hours could sometimes take all day. In 1984 I was making my first trip to Andalusia, travelling by the classic main line from Madrid to Cordoba, Malaga and Algeciras at the southern tip of Spain. The first day should have been a straightforward journey from my home in Kent to Paris, crossing the Channel by ship from Dover to Calais, before catching the overnight sleeper to Madrid. The crossing itself was superb, with the sea calm on a sparkling February day, and just a light sea haze. On arrival at Calais, all foot passengers were bundled onto a bus and whisked off to Customs, some way from the Gare Maritime, forcing those of us travelling on by train to manhandle our luggage back to the station. In those days, this kind of experience was not untypical of the poor treatment of passengers transferring between ship and train.

From the start, British passengers made a major contribution to the success of the Wagons-Lits network. In the 1880s and '90s, a number of sleeper services, including the Rome Express and the Méditerranée Express, were extended beyond Paris to operate to and from Calais in order to connect with cross-Channel shipping services. On Fridays, the Peninsular and Oriental Express left Calais for Brindisi, in southern Italy, from where connections by steamer were available to Port Said and Cairo. After the opening of the Simplon Tunnel in 1906, a Calais–Venice car was attached to the service from Paris.

Despite two world wars, the depression of the 1930s and post-war austerity, British patronage was able to sustain Calais' key role in the sleeper network well into the twentieth century. As late as 1969, for example, direct sleepers still ran daily from Calais Maritime to Milan and to San Remo on Italy's Ligurian coast via Marseille, Nice and the French Riviera. In Paris, the Calais–Milan sleeper was attached to the Direct Orient Express, which at that time conveyed a sleeping car from Paris to Istanbul, Athens or Sofia, depending on which day of the week it was. During the winter sports season, sleepers still left Calais for Innsbruck, Interlaken and Chur. In 1972's summer timetable, through sleepers from Calais

A view of Calais Maritime station, taken from a cross-Channel ferry. (Author, 1988)

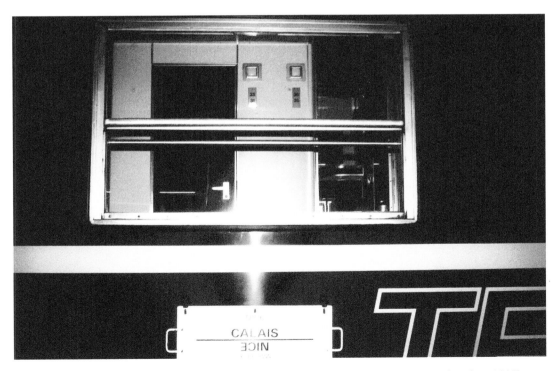

A close-up view of the Nice–Calais sleeper in the Flandres–Riviera Express. (Author, 1988)

The Calais portion of the Flandres–Riviera near Wimille, with the two blue sleeping cars marshalled immediately behind the locomotives. (Michel Ledieu, 1989)

Night trains boarding at Paris Gare d'Austerlitz, point of departure for the Paris–Madrid Talgo. (Pascal Poggi, 2012)

ran daily to Milan, San Remo, Venice and Innsbruck, the latter joining up at Basle with the Paris–Vienna cars of the Arlberg Express.

Over the years the range of destinations served by direct sleepers from Calais gradually fell away until there was just one all-year-round service left – Calais–Nice, a shortened version of the former service to San Remo. However, this was just one portion of a quite remarkable train called the Flandres-Riviera, an overnight service linking several points in northern France and the Low Countries with the south of France. In addition to the Calais–Nice, this train included sleeping cars from Brussels and Tourcoing to Ventimiglia. There were also couchettes from Calais to Nice, Amsterdam to Ventimiglia, Brussels to Ventimiglia and Tourcoing to Ventimiglia. All these portions were joined together at the Gare du Nord in Paris to form a single train to the south. Seating coaches from Calais and Amsterdam and restaurant cars from Calais and Brussels were detached at Paris, so the whole operation was fiendishly complex. In the winter 1987/88 timetable, for example, the Amsterdam/Brussels cars arrived at the Gare du Nord at 22.06; the Tourcoing cars at 22.14; and the Calais cars at 22.28. Once shunting operations were complete, the combined train left for the Riviera at 23.12 – more than an hour after the Amsterdam/Brussels cars had arrived. Calais Maritime station closed in 1994 with the start of Eurostar services through the Channel Tunnel, although the Flandres-Riviera itself continued for a few years, using Calais Ville station instead of Calais Maritime.

Paris–Madrid Talgo

My onward train journey from Calais to Paris was uneventful, but, on transferring from the Gare du Nord to the Gare d'Austerlitz, I was in for a shock. The sleeper to Madrid was '*supprimé*'; or, in plain English, 'cancelled'. I stared incredulously at the departure indicator and looked for another screen to confirm that it was not just a malfunction, but there it was, in black and white. Almost before I had started, my plans and itinerary seemed to lie in ruins. I rushed to the travel centre just as it was about to close for the day to see what could be done. From the deepest recesses of my memory I summoned up my best French to explain my problem. To my great relief, the clerk was well-briefed and immediately offered a number of options: travel to Irun by that night's sleeper and then on to Madrid by day; travel by day trains the next day; or catch the next night's Paris–Madrid Talgo. Having almost no time to weigh up the pros and cons of each option, I decided to accept the offer of a compartment on the following night's Talgo. The clerk transferred my reservation quickly and at no cost and I was overcome by a wave of relief that such a major problem had been so smoothly resolved. The reason for the cancellation? Basque separatists had blown up a short section of track in Spain. I reassured myself that they would not strike again two nights running.

In its long history, the overnight service between Paris and Madrid was no stranger to disruption by conflict of one sort or another, notably during the Spanish Civil War in the 1930s and the Second World War in the 1940s. Now another conflict had intervened, and at that moment the struggle for Basque independence was suddenly my least favourite political cause. I was faced with the hassle of finding a hotel room and changing some of my pesetas into francs – back in 1984, credit cards were not widely accepted in much of Europe – and I also needed to find a way of salvaging as much of my itinerary as possible. The Hotel Terminus-Austerlitz opposite the station solved the first problem and a bureau de change was not hard to find. Having successfully negotiated what had been a catastrophic start to my trip, I wound down over a pleasant and relaxing dinner in Le Grenadier, the station restaurant, and contemplated what I would do with an unanticipated twenty-four hours in Paris.

The first sleeper services between Paris and Madrid were introduced in 1887 following the completion of the railway from Madrid to Irun and across the border to Hendaye, in France. In fact, because of the difference in track gauge between France and Spain, passengers had to take one sleeper from Paris to Irun and complete the journey to Madrid the next night in a second sleeper train. This was the route of the Sud Express, a train that, until 1895, continued on from Madrid to Lisbon, thus fulfilling one of the grandest ambitions of the Compagnie Internationale des Wagons-Lits by linking St Petersburg, then the capital of Russia, with Lisbon and the transatlantic steamship trade. In this grand plan, passengers travelled by the Nord Express from Russia to Paris and then onwards by its southern twin, the Sud Express. In 1900 schedules were improved so that the French train became a daytime train de luxe and passengers could make the journey to Madrid in a day and a night rather than over two nights. The French train retained its luxury Pullman cars right into the 1960s, offering a superior restaurant service compared even with that available to passengers in the ordinary first-class carriages.

The year 1969 saw the introduction of the Puerta del Sol – the first genuine through service between Paris and Madrid. This was made possible by the installation of equipment at the border that enabled the wheelsets of carriages to be adjusted, thus allowing the sleeping cars to run on both the French and Spanish systems. Passengers using the sleepers from Paris to Madrid no longer had to change trains, unlike those in the ordinary seating coaches, which were still first class only. Separate restaurant cars were provided on the French and Spanish sections of the journey. In that year the name Sud Express became confined to the separate overnight train from Paris to Lisbon. While through couchette cars were introduced to operate over the entire route, the Sud's sleeping cars ran only between Irun and Lisbon. In the 1980s, the Portuguese sleepers used on the Sud had the distinction of being the oldest still operating in Western Europe, being of the S2U class built in 1926–27.

In 1981 a brand new purpose-built train of articulated air-conditioned coaches, the Paris–Madrid Talgo, was introduced. Like its companion, the Barcelona Talgo, this new train consisted entirely of sleeping and restaurant vehicles, which could run in both France and Spain. The cancellation of the Paris–Madrid Talgo had left me stranded in Paris, but in the end it was not difficult to decide how to spend an unexpected day in the French capital. After breakfast I wandered around this most beautiful of cities, with character on every corner, and then surrendered to a delicious afternoon of pleasure in the fleshpots, where my natural English reserve seemed to go down well with my new Gallic friends.

At a quarter to eight, I presented myself once again at Austerlitz station and this time found to my great relief the squat Talgo train humming gently at the platform ready for

The Paris–Madrid Talgo on the direct Madrid–Burgos line (now disused). (Torrego family, 1990)

Madrid Chamartin station, the destination of the Paris–Madrid Talgo. (M. Peinado [CC BY- 2.0] via Wikimedia Commons, 2008*)

Sleeping car tickets for journeys on the Night Ferry (top), Paris–Madrid Talgo (centre) and Nord Express (bottom). (Author's collection)

A towel and a small bar of soap were provided for each sleeping car passenger – two each for those travelling in first-class singles or specials. The soap wrappers came in various styles, and here are some from France, Spain, Sweden and Norway. (Author's collection)

its 1,500 km overnight journey to Madrid. I was welcomed on board, shown to my sleeping compartment, and felt a small sense of triumph that I was at last en route to Spain. As I had eaten only a standard French breakfast and skipped lunch, I was anxious to sample the delights of the restaurant car and went along for dinner as soon as seemed decent, given the Spanish tendency to eat very late. I was directed to a vacant table from where I could peer into the vast empty darkness of the French countryside, which was punctuated by the lights of the occasional farmhouse or village as the train rattled along. The fixed menu was sumptuous: soup, main course, cheese and dessert. I retired to bed in a state of complete satisfaction after the exertions of the day.

Over the years I used the Paris–Madrid Talgo several times. After the cancellation in 1984, I was hoping for better luck when I tried it again the following year. It was not to be. To make the most of the first day, I had decided to travel out via Belgium. When I reached Brussels I discovered that the train for Paris was running more than an hour late, having awaited the Moscow–Paris sleepers of the Ost-West Express, which had been badly delayed by severe winter weather in Byelorussia over twenty-four hours earlier. So here I was in Belgium, en route from England to Spain, delayed by bad weather in the Soviet Union. It was a nail-biting journey and I eventually arrived at the Gare d'Austerlitz just in time to see the tail light of the sleeper to Madrid gliding out of the platform. I had missed it and was stranded ... again. Fortunately, once again the ticket office clerk was very helpful and, fully grasping the implications of bad weather in Byelorussia for onward travel to Spain, re-booked me on the following night's Talgo without any fuss.

So, another night's enforced stay at the Hotel Terminus-Austerlitz and Sunday at large in the French capital. As the time drew near for me to catch the Paris-Madrid Talgo, I retrieved my bags from left luggage and kept my fingers crossed that my sleeper reservation had been successfully transferred. It had. Knowing that high standards were expected of the clientele using the restaurant car, I changed into my suit and went in search of dinner. A few passengers were already seated. No sooner had I entered the diner than I was greeted effusively by the Spanish chief steward with 'How are you? Nice to see you again', as he showed me to my table. Either he had a phenomenal memory, remembering me from the year before, or else he had mistaken me for someone else. Either way, it put me in the right frame of mind to enjoy a fine four-course meal, which, with aperitif, wine, liqueur and coffee, cost around £20 – a bargain.

In 1992 the Paris–Madrid Talgo was renamed Francisco de Goya, and in 1997 the rolling stock was replaced by a hotel train offering superior accommodation, including some *gran classe* compartments with their own shower and toilet facilities. On the opening of the new cross-border high-speed line from Perpignan to Barcelona in 2013, the Trenhotels from Paris to Barcelona and Madrid were both withdrawn. Passengers from Paris to Madrid are now recommended to travel by day train, changing in Barcelona. This is a journey that can now be done in around ten hours, but there are no direct or overnight services. Until 2017 passengers could still take a couchette from Paris to Irun on the overnight Palombe Bleue, completing the journey to Madrid by day train, but even this option has now been withdrawn. Of the Wagons-Lits company's grand scheme to link St Petersburg with Lisbon, the Sud Express is now the sole relic, operating as a hotel train between Irun and Lisbon.

Andalusia

Back to 1984 ... having reached Madrid a day late, I needed to get back on track and head for Cordoba. I had just over half an hour to cross from Chamartin to Atocha station, with little expectation of achieving this in a city with which I was unfamiliar. Nevertheless, by some miracle, at 09.30 I found myself ensconced in my reserved window seat as the express departed on the five and a half hour journey south to Cordoba. Whereas Paris had been in the grip of a freezing cold snap, knots of wild flowers were in full bloom by the lineside here. In twelve hours I had been transported from winter to spring. The train passed through places with names that were familiar, bestowing a tangible reality on locations that had previously been merely constructs of the mind: Aranjuez, inspiration for a famous guitar concerto by Rodrigo, and Alcazar de San Juan in La Mancha, with its traditional windmills on a nearby hill, inspiration for a defining story about Don Quixote.

At Cordoba, I stepped out of the air-conditioned carriage into a wall of heat. The blue skies and warmth of this February afternoon in Andalusia would have been regarded as a fine summer's day in England. I left the station and its tall palm trees and walked a short distance along a dusty road to a modern hotel. (Returning to Cordoba in 2011, I found the area totally transformed with high-rise hotels and other buildings dominating the landscape, the old traditional station replaced with a large new one whose platforms are in a kind of concrete cavern, and the dusty road of 1984 now buried under a six-lane highway.)

Before the internet made it all so easy, obtaining information about southern Europe usually meant visiting the relevant national tourist office in London. You would tell the counter clerk – often an elegant middle-aged woman with a cardigan draped over her shoulders and enveloped in a haze of perfume – what you wanted and she would disappear before returning with a leaflet or booklet which you hoped would a) be relevant, and b) give you the barest outline of what was interesting or, more usually, what was not, all the while feeling slightly guilty at having put such a grand personage to the trouble of fetching it for you. From the information I had managed to obtain, I knew that the Great Mosque and the old town were worth seeing, so I set off in that general direction.

There are some places you visit for the first time as a traveller that turn out to be rather humdrum, many that are mildly interesting, and a few that just take your breath away. Cordoba is a knockout. My first impressions were of an elegant city with wide boulevards, broad open spaces lined with orange trees laden with fruit, and tall palms providing a degree of shade. At the Alcazar, the palace of the Catholic monarchs Ferdinand and Isabella, there were tranquil public gardens. Then I discovered the old town, a maze of narrow streets and alleyways barely wide enough for two people to pass. At every corner ornamental gates led to the courtyards of private houses, often giving a glimpse of an exotic sub-tropical garden within.

At the heart of the old city stands the Great Mosque. Initially constructed between the eighth and tenth centuries, its conversion to a Catholic cathedral began in the thirteenth after the re-conquest of Cordoba by Christian kings. The scale of the building is vast, reflecting the size and importance of Cordoba under Islamic rule, when it is thought there

The train shed at Madrid Atocha station, before it was converted into a passenger concourse. (Smiley.toerist. (File: Madrid Atocha 1981) [CC BY-SA 3.0] via Wikimedia Commons, 1981*)

Three types of sleeping car (Lx, P and YFT) can be seen on this night train from Almeria at Madrid Atocha station. (Torrego family, 1987)

The charming old station at Cordoba, since replaced with a functional modern building on a different site. (Author, 1984)

The mesmerising sequence of columns and arches at Cordoba's Great Mosque. (Bert Kaufmann, 2010)

were half a million inhabitants, making it perhaps the largest city in Europe at that time. The interior of the mosque is intricately decorated, the most striking feature being the seemingly endless rows of marble columns supporting arches of alternating red and white stonework, creating a stunning visual effect. Shafts of sunlight shining through windows and other openings create pools of coloured or white light on floors and walls, or highlight spectacular decorative features so that they stand out in the subdued light of the interior. The mosque at Cordoba is one of the great man-made spaces of the world, although these days the throng of tourists is so overwhelming that it might be difficult to experience the atmosphere of what is a holy place for both Christians and Muslims. In 1984, I had it almost to myself.

Next day I took a lunchtime train to Malaga. Although the distance from Cordoba to Malaga is less than 200 km, the journey was slow in the days before the new AVE line. However, what it lacked in speed, it made up for in terms of scenery. On the southern part of the route after Bobadilla, the line passed through a spectacular gorge, with the train proceeding with great caution as it threaded its way precariously along the edge of a river under overhanging rocks. Sadly, this original line to Malaga closed to passengers in 2013.

Malaga is dominated by the Gibralfaro, a massive fourteenth-century fortification built under Islamic rule. From here there are spectacular views of the harbour, the Mediterranean Sea, the city and the surrounding hills. I was shocked to find this historic site in a ruinous state. The massive timber gates of the main entrance were rotting away, unsecured and swinging in the wind, while the supporting brickwork and masonry were crumbling. The huge open spaces inside the fortifications were unkempt and weed-infested and the battlements were in poor condition. Only the gardens surrounding the fort seemed to be looked after and were colourful, charming and full of atmosphere as the fading light heralded a spectacular sunset.

The following morning I set off on the last leg of my outward journey. From the bright and airy station at Malaga, I retraced my steps as far as the important, if isolated, junction station of Bobadilla, where I changed trains for the three-hour ride to my ultimate destination – Algeciras. It was another superb journey following the course of rivers through mountain scenery. Under the bright blue sky, the colours were vivid – rich red earth, deep greens and blues, the landscape peppered with fruiting orange and lemon trees. On-train refreshments were provided by a casually dressed man carrying a basket of rolls in one hand and a bucket containing cans of beer in the other. It was unclear whether he was contracted to provide this service or whether this was just a bit of local private enterprise unofficially exploiting a market opportunity. Either way, the *bocadillo* was delicious and the beer very welcome. The train called at the station for Ronda, an ancient city located on top of two rocky outcrops, linked together by an arched stone bridge towering 120 metres above the canyon that separates the two parts of the city. As the line looped around the valley below in order to lose height, this spectacular bridge remained visible for miles.

It is easy to think of Algeciras as being at the end of Europe, but in fact it is just as much a gateway to Africa. Ferries link the busy harbour with the Spanish enclaves of Ceuta and Melilla on the northern shore of Africa. Just across the bay from Algeciras lies the British dependency of Gibraltar, dominated by the Rock, the last outpost of British sovereign territory on the European mainland. I had eight hours to explore Algeciras before starting my two-day journey home. I found it to be a pleasant city of whitewashed houses and charming narrow alleyways, with palms and orange trees in profusion. The railway station was modern and striking in design, with the use of blue and yellow features against a plain white background.

Iberia Express

Already standing in Algeciras station from late afternoon were the two sleeping cars for that night's train to Madrid, resplendent in traditional midnight blue and gold. Marshalled next to them was a through couchette coach to Paris. This carriage would take two nights to make the journey of 1,316 miles, and was itself the successor of an Algeciras–Hendaye sleeping car introduced in 1897 to provide a land route between London and Gibraltar and between Paris and France's North African colonies. Somehow, its continued existence seemed like a faint echo of the importance of British and French patronage for European night trains in the long-dead age of empire, although in truth its passengers in 1984 were more likely to be North Africans travelling to Paris than Brits or Frenchmen returning home from the former colonies. The through couchette to Paris was withdrawn in 1993, but the Algeciras–Madrid sleeper survived until the opening of the Cordoba–Malaga high-speed line in 2007.

When the time came for me to board, the sleeping car conductor at first refused to accept my reservation and needed some persuading that it was genuine. Admittedly, the handwritten tickets and reservations issued by Thomas Cook in London were no doubt confusing and unfamiliar, but eventually he realised that the name on the tickets corresponded to the name on his passenger list. Profoundly relieved not to find myself stranded at the southern tip of Spain, I was at last granted access to my compartment, ordered a celebratory gin and tonic and spent a very comfortable night tucked up in bed for the thirteen-hour journey to Madrid.

Arrival at Madrid's Chamartin station was scheduled for just after 11 a.m. It is a measure of just how slow transit times used to be on Spain's railways that a thirteen-hour journey from Algeciras to Madrid in the centre of the country was then followed by a nine-hour journey north to the French frontier. Spain's topography and geography meant that the original broad-gauge network was built using circuitous routes to circumvent the many mountain ranges and avoid steep gradients. Since the 1990s, the new AVE network has revolutionised rail travel in Spain, with powerful trains on high-speed lines that steer a direct course through mountain ranges and over or under other geographical obstacles.

From Madrid I caught the Iberia Express: destination Hendaye, just inside France. This offered the luxury of a fixed-price lunch in the restaurant car, to which I added an aperitif, some wine and a coffee, and returned to my seat suitably replete. However, as the day wore on, it dawned on me that I would have no time for dinner on reaching Hendaye before boarding my onward sleeper to Paris, and I was reluctantly forced to the conclusion that I would need to return to the restaurant car in the evening and have the same meal

It's 10.15 a.m. at Cordoba station. The Barcelona–Seville sleeper is about to begin the last stage of its long overnight journey. (Author, 1984)

Malaga's old terminus before the new AVE high-speed line was built. The staff and passengers seem to be casting a critical eye on Picasso's painting *Guernica*, which is on display at the end of the platform. (Author, 1984)

The luxury tourist train Al Andalus takes the curves near Almargen on the line to Algeciras. (Miguel López Galán, 2017)

The spectacular bridge over the gorge at Ronda. (Pedro J. Pacheco [CC BY-SA 3.0] via Wikimedia Commons, 2014*)

Above: End of the line – the cool and colourful station at Algeciras. (Author, 1984)

Right: Algeciras – a charming alleyway lined with orange trees. (Author, 1984)

all over again. So, at 7 p.m., somewhat to the astonishment of the other passengers in my compartment, I announced that I was going for dinner, an absurdly early hour for an evening meal in Spain. The staff in the restaurant car were equally bemused and apologised for the fact that they could offer me only the same menu that I had eaten six hours earlier. However, that was not going to put this greedy Englishman off his dinner, so I chose a better quality wine and replaced the aperitif with a brandy to follow the meal. After all, I was going to need something to aid the digestion of two identical meals in one day.

At Hendaye, La Palombe Bleue was already in the platform with my compartment in a familiar T2-type sleeper. The pleasant conductor served me a nightcap and took my order for breakfast. The final day of this journey was almost a reverse of the first, but this time without the trauma. From the Gare d'Austerlitz, I took Metro line 5 to the Gare du Nord and caught the boat train to Calais for the ferry to Folkestone. The warmth and blue skies of Andalusia were now just a pleasant memory as I wrapped up in sweater and scarf to brave the cold of a gloomy February afternoon in Kent.

Turn right for Dover – the waiting room for ferry passengers at Calais Maritime. (Author, 1984)

Two T2-type sleeping cars for Madrid await their passengers at Algeciras. (Author, 1984)

Preserved YF-type sleeper No. 4648 at Aranda de Duero. (Miguel López Galán, 2014)

To Portugal

Paris–Madrid Talgo: Third Time Lucky!

My first visit to Portugal in 1989 would take me from Madrid to Lisbon on a night train called Lusitania. This did not fill me with confidence as the liner of that name was torpedoed in the First World War with huge loss of life. The train might just as well have been called Titanic as far as I was concerned. For once, I decided to avoid the usual difficulties that so often came with my more complex starts, such as having to make a last-minute dash across Paris to catch my sleeper, and instead settled for a straightforward hovercraft crossing from Dover to Boulogne and then a connecting train to Paris.

At the Gare d'Austerlitz, I was relieved to find the Paris–Madrid Talgo sitting in the platform. Both of my previous attempts to catch this train had ended in disaster; the first time because it was cancelled after terrorists blew up a section of track in Spain, the second time because I missed it after being on a train that had been delayed by bad weather – in the Soviet Union! Travelling to Spain this way was a civilised affair, with the twelve and a half hour journey allowing plenty of time to enjoy dinner in the restaurant car, a full night's sleep, and breakfast the next morning, but it cost enough to make me wonder why anyone would bother. Taking the Talgo had to be one of the most expensive train rides in Europe; in 1989 the supplement for a single compartment ran out at over £91 one way on top of the first-class fare. Even so, there seemed to be no shortage of customers even in February – mostly Spanish and French, of course, but there were also a fair few British and some Americans and Far Eastern tourists as well.

The Talgo's excellent restaurant car – full to capacity on this occasion – provided a sumptuous dinner as the express charged southwards through the night. The five-course menu – soup, fish, meat, cheese and dessert, accompanied by a large sherry, half a bottle of Spanish red, coffee and a large cognac – cost just £19 and sent me to bed feeling like a plutocrat. Breakfast was taken as the sun came up over the dramatic snow-capped Sierra de Guadarrama.

In the final months of operation before withdrawal, the hotel train 'Francisco de Goya' passes through the suburbs of Paris en route to Madrid. (Torrego family, 2013)

Upholding the finest traditions of the Paris–Madrid Talgo, dinner is served in the restaurant car of its successor, Francisco de Goya. (Torrego family, 2013)

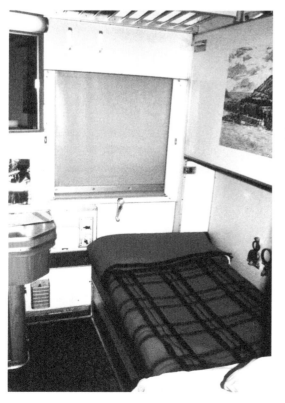

Above: Sleeping car No. 4690 at Madrid Chamartin on the Estrella Lusitania to Lisbon. (Author, 1989)

Left: This compartment on the Estrella Lusitania is set up for single occupancy, with the upper berth folded away behind the picture (top right). The washstand is on the left with the mirror located above it. The window blind (centre) provides privacy at night. (Author, 1989)

Estrella Lusitania

The night train from Madrid's Chamartin station to Lisbon, the Estrella Lusitania, included two gleaming sleeping cars dating from the 1960s in traditional Wagons-Lits livery – deep blue lined out in gold. The International Sleeping Car Company introduced a Madrid–Lisbon service in 1884. The original coaches had fourteen berths in compartments and four more in the corridor to take advantage of the wide Spanish gauge. During the daytime, the corridor berths could be reconfigured as eight armchairs. From 1887 the Madrid–Lisbon sleepers became part of the Sud Express, which, with its counterpart the Nord Express, provided a means of travelling by luxury trains with sleeping cars all the way from St Petersburg in pre-revolutionary Russia via Paris to Lisbon. Advertised connections by steamship were available from Lisbon to Cape Town, Madeira and South America.

In 1895 the Sud was rerouted over a more direct line, which avoided the Spanish capital, so a separate Madrid–Lisbon train was introduced to replace it. Bradshaw's August 1914 Continental Guide shows the first-class-only sleeper train running three nights a week, leaving Madrid just after 11 p.m. and arriving at Lisbon well after two o'clock in the afternoon. From the outset the route was via Caceres and Valencia de Alcantara, and remained so until 2008, when the train was rerouted via Salamanca on account of the poor condition of the track on the cross-border section of the original route, which was subsequently closed. Lusitania became a hotel train in 1995 and continues to run between the two capitals under its historic name. The change of route has once again allowed Lusitania to run together with the Sud Express for most of the journey and they operate as a single train between Medina del Campo and Lisbon.

With white sheets and red tartan blanket, my bed had already been made up and the compartment was as neat as a new pin. However, the train gave my dinner a good shaking about as the sleeper picked up speed on the broad-gauge track. Customs arrangements on the Spanish–Portuguese border were rather more formal than elsewhere at land frontiers in what was then the European Economic Community. Passports were examined carefully by both sets of officials and all passengers were asked whether they had anything to declare. Even passengers in the sleeping cars were not spared this ritual at 6.15 a.m. Another peculiarity was the time difference between the two countries, which meant that on paper the train arrived in Portugal before it had left Spain.

Sleep eluded me after the border formalities so I left the Estrella Lusitania at Entroncamento, a major junction around 100 km north of Lisbon. 'Entroncamento' just means 'Junction', but it would be rude of me to suggest that there had been a collective failure of imagination when deciding on a name for the place. It is just as well I knew what time the train was due to arrive as there was not a single sign on any platform to tell you where you were. Arrival was just after dawn and the station seemed deserted. I wondered what I would do with my two hours between trains, but in the event there was plenty to keep me entertained.

Although a busy junction, there was no footbridge or subway linking the platforms, so, as is often the case on the Continent, your safety is your own lookout as you cross the tracks. The low morning sun gradually lit up the traditional yellow and white station buildings while the canopies provided deep shade for the platforms. Meanwhile, the station had become a hive of activity, with hundreds of students arriving and departing. They swarmed carelessly over platforms and tracks alike, seemingly heedless of the danger to life and limb as friends were greeted and gossip exchanged. If a train was at the platform, they would simply board through the nearest door and exit straight out on to the tracks the other side. If the train started to move while they were on board they would make a quick exit. The station staff seemed unconcerned about what was clearly a daily occurrence and fortunately there did not seem to be any casualties. Just after eight o'clock, the Sud Express arrived on the last leg of its journey to Lisbon from Irun on the French border. For me this was a train of some interest as it conveyed not only a couchette car from Paris – a journey of over twenty-four hours – but also one of the oldest sleeping cars still in daily use on any European railway, the Irun–Lisbon sleeper, built in 1926–27.

As nine o'clock approached, I began to prepare myself for the next stage of my journey. Entroncamento is quite a large station, with numerous tracks, but I could not establish which platform my train would leave from. The printed departure sheets gave no clue; there were no departure indicators of any description; and such announcements as there were seemed indecipherable. I could not even rely on gravitating to a platform where a crowd of passengers was waiting. Now that the students had gone, I seemed to be pretty much on my own again. I was reduced to peering into the distance until eventually I saw a train approaching. Then all I had to do was guess which platform it was heading for, gather my belongings and run across the tracks in the hope of getting there before the train did. I guessed right.

From the Atlantic to the Mediterranean

After visiting Lisbon, with its Old World charm and ancient trams, I began a transit right across Iberia from the Atlantic coast of Portugal to Valencia on the Mediterranean coast of Spain. I returned to Entroncamento and boarded a local train to Badajoz, just across the border in Spain. This journey was a pure delight. In dazzling sunshine, the lightly loaded train proceeded with no great sense of urgency through pleasant countryside, halting at gleaming whitewashed wayside stations with their characteristic blue wall tiles, all the while losing time and taking more than three hours for the 166 km journey – four hours if you add in the time difference between Spain and Portugal. There were few towns of any size, the largest being Portalegre, which was just visible in the distance from the station of the same name.

At Elvas, the last station before the border, all passengers were required to disembark for passport control. As there were now only two of us, the official scrutinised my passport carefully, checked it against a massive tome presumably listing lost passports and persons of interest, and finally stamped it with a flourish. Once back on the train, it was time for the customs examination, which was a more cursory affair. On arrival at Badajoz, both of us were once again directed to passport examination and then through the specially built customs hall. The formality and officiousness of the whole procedure for just two passengers could have been a scene from some ancient Ealing film comedy, so it seems entirely in keeping with the slightly farcical nature of the operation that passenger trains on the line were withdrawn in 2004, reinstated in 2009, closed again in 2012 and reinstated again in 2017. I hope there are at least a few remaining passengers who have kept faith

Above: Rush hour at Entroncamento station. (Author, 1989)

Right: Boarding the Sud Express in its heyday. (Gulbenkian Art Foundation Library*)

Narrow winding streets barely wide enough for an ancient tram to squeeze through – the charms of Lisbon. (Milica Vujicic, 2015)

Sleeping car No. 4652 on the Guadiana Express at Badajoz. (Author, 1993)

with this on-off service, although this seems unlikely as it now consists of a single daily train in each direction.

Fortunately I was in no hurry. I had almost four hours to spare in Badajoz before my sleeper departed for Madrid, so I left my suitcase at the station and went off to explore this ancient city, with its fine Gateway of the Palms and castle set on a hill. Seen from a distance rising above the surrounding trees, the towers and spires of the Badajoz skyline glowed majestically in the early evening sun. Wandering about the town without a map or guidebook, I found myself outside a large whitewashed tenement, some of whose houses were in a ruinous state. With my briefcase, sports jacket and camera, I immediately attracted the attention of a crowd of children playing in the street. They surrounded me, bombarding me with questions that I could neither understand nor answer. While I tried to take a photograph, one very small boy grabbed hold of my briefcase, which I had placed on the ground, but it was so full of books, reports and camera equipment that he could barely lift it. Everyone burst out laughing. The children asked me to take a photograph of them, which I did, but by then the light had faded so they appeared only as ghostly shapes outlined against the tenement behind.

By the time I returned to the station it was around seven o'clock and getting dark. Having had only a light breakfast and sandwich lunch, I was feeling hungry, so I went in search of a restaurant for dinner. Try as I might, I could not find anywhere that was open. It eventually became obvious that I was not going to get any dinner before my train departed and that I would probably be found starved to death the next morning in my sleeping compartment. There can be few more desolate souls than a hungry Englishman deprived of his dinner. I made do with a bar of chocolate and a can of beer, followed by a rumbling tummy and a thoroughly bad mood.

My comfortable compartment on the Guadiana Express should have enabled me to get a good night's sleep on the ten-hour journey back to Madrid, but the ride was one of the worst I ever had in a Continental sleeping car, as well as one of the noisiest, as the vehicle was marshalled next to a diesel loco. Until 1975 the Badajoz–Madrid sleeper operated via Caceres under the name Extremadura Express – Extremadura being the remote border region where Badajoz is located. The train was then re-routed via Ciudad Real, south of Madrid. Shortly before my journey in 1989, the train had been renamed Guadiana Express after the river on which Badajoz stands, which marks the border between Spain and Portugal. In 1993 the Guadiana reverted to the Caceres route, but by 1995 it was running only three days a week and had lost its name. The following year it vanished from the timetable, effectively made redundant by faster daytime Badajoz–Madrid services, which were able to use the new high-speed AVE line for part of the journey.

On arrival at Madrid's Chamartin station I was desperate for something to eat, and not only enjoyed breakfast, but also bought lunch to take with me on the train to Valencia. Still hungry after missing dinner the previous evening, it took monumental willpower to resist eating it long before lunchtime. From Chamartin I caught a local train to Madrid's other main terminus, Atocha. This had temporarily been renamed Mediodía as a new, much larger Atocha was then under construction in preparation for the AVE high-speed line to Seville, which would begin operating in 1992. Mediodía turned out to be Atocha's low-level station, used mostly by suburban trains, temporarily adapted to deal with main-line expresses. Although Atocha was a vast building site, this did not excuse the almost total lack of information. There were no departure sheets and the electronic indicators seemed to be updated as and when the operator saw fit. For example, the 08.50 to Alicante – the principal business train of the day – was not shown on the departure board until it actually rolled into the station, whereupon there was a great rush of immaculately dressed señores and señoras desperately trying to preserve their dignity as they scrambled to reach the right platform before the train departed without them.

My 09.15 train to Valencia via Cuenca was still missing from the departure indicator at nine o'clock so I went to look for it. By chance the indicator for Platform 2 showed it departing from there, but this was occupied by a very long suburban unit with its doors wide open. The unwary could have climbed aboard. The Valencia train in fact turned out to be a rather smart three-coach diesel unit positioned right at the far end of the platform. In the bright sunshine, the journey across some of Spain's emptiest landscapes was a stunning ride through arid rocky terrain with spectacular gorges and hills before descending to the fertile coastal strip at Valencia, Spain's third largest city. Valencia Norte station is a treat – a celebration of the orange, a motif exuberantly and ubiquitously displayed on the colourful façade and in the wonderful art nouveau booking hall. I had taken just one shot of this highly photogenic station when I was approached by a friendly police officer who asked me to stop. I did not argue.

Valencia to Paris

The next morning I began my two-day journey home with a four-hour ride north along the Mediterranean coast line to Barcelona. Britain's two main railways from London to Scotland are called the East and West Coast Main Lines, although, in reality, any glimpses of the coastline are relatively fleeting, especially on the West Coast route. By contrast, it is possible to travel from Valencia in Spain, along the Mediterranean coast of France and right round Italy to Ravenna on the Adriatic with the coastline in view more often than not. For most of the way from Valencia to Barcelona, the train passes along a flat coastal strip amid countless orange trees, statuesque palms and, in February, cherry trees in full blossom. This area is also given over to market gardening and the orange-coloured soil is here and there divided into small plots with perfectly straight rows of lettuces, radicchios and other colourful produce.

At Barcelona I had several hours to explore before my sleeper to Paris. The city was preparing to host the 1992 Olympic Games and seemed transformed since my first visit in 1974 into an altogether more confident, cleaner and livelier place – a reputation that the Games have cemented in the world's collective consciousness right up to the present day. I spent the afternoon ascending the monument to Columbus and then riding the cable car from the port area across the city's skyline to Montjuic. It was a fabulous way to get a bird's-eye view of this wonderful city, whose suburbs spread as far as the lower slopes of the surrounding hills. Then it was back to Sants station for the 21.00 Barcelona Talgo to Paris, which was in every respect the equal of its Madrid–Paris counterpart. In my view, these two trains represented the best in overnight rail travel in Western Europe in the 1980s. Both were all-sleeper trains that took at least twelve hours to make the transit with few intermediate stops, allowing plenty of time to enjoy an excellent dinner before retiring for a long night's rest.

The magnificent façade of Madrid Atocha station. (Luis Garcia [CC BY-SA 4.0] via Wikimedia Commons, 2015*)

The former train shed at Atocha, now transformed into a spectacular passenger concourse in the guise of a tropical palm house. (Daderot (Own work) [Public Domain] via Wikimedia Commons, 2008*)

The symmetrical façade of Valencia Norte station. (Diego Delso [CC BY-SA 4.0] via Wikimedia Commons, 2014*)

In praise of the orange – the art nouveau booking hall of Valencia Norte station. (Dorico (Own work) [CC BY-SA 3.0] via Wikimedia Commons, 2013*)

See Barcelona by cable car! (Andrew Bone, 2016)

The Paris–Barcelona sleeper train 'Joan Miró' at Figueres near journey's end. (Jordi Verdugo [CC BY-SA 2.0] via Wikimedia Commons, 2012*)

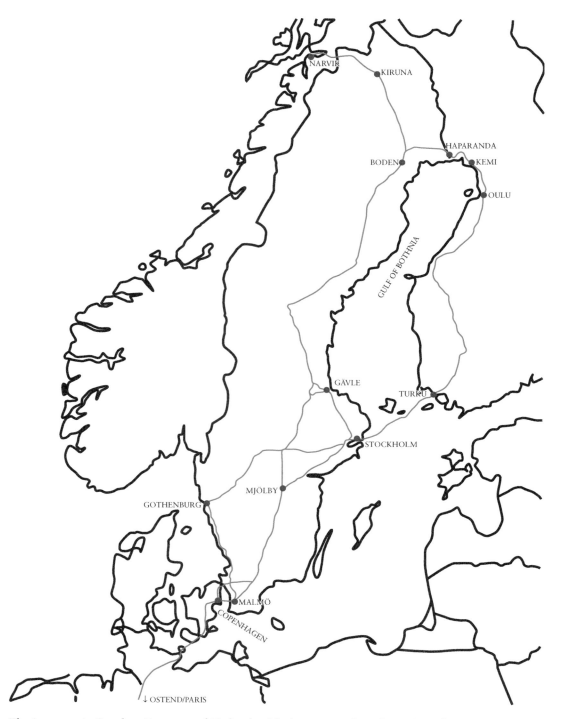

The journeys in Sweden, Norway and Finland, with the routes taken shown in red.

To Arctic Sweden and Norway

Nord Express

'You must be mad' was the general consensus of opinion among friends and work colleagues. It was November 1986 and I was heading for the Arctic. The hours of daylight in northern Sweden and Norway would be short and the weather freezing. I was travelling just about as far north as it is possible to go by rail in Western Europe, virtually the whole length of Sweden, then across to Narvik in Norway. Much of the journey would be in sleepers, with the only two nights on terra firma being spent inside the Arctic Circle.

It was in 1981 that I first encountered the night train that I would come to use more than any other – the Nord Express to Copenhagen. The main section of the train departed from Paris, but conveniently for me and any other British traveller minded to use it, there was a through sleeper from Ostend, which joined up with the Paris portion at Liège. The Nord Express was inaugurated in 1896 by the Compagnie Internationale des Wagons-Lits. Starting from Paris Gare du Nord and Ostend, it travelled via Brussels, Cologne, Hanover, Berlin and Königsberg (now Kaliningrad) to Saint Petersburg, the then capital of Imperial Russia. It was part of a plan by Wagons-Lits to establish a direct link between Saint Petersburg and Lisbon to connect with ocean liners to America. In Paris there was a connecting service to the Sud Express for Lisbon. The Russian Revolution of 1917 spelled the end for the Saint Petersburg service, so when the train was reinstated after the First World War, it was diverted to Warsaw and Riga instead. After the Second World War the 'Iron Curtain' put an end to the service as originally conceived. However, the pre-war train had occasionally included through cars to Copenhagen, so the name Nord Express was transferred to the night train from Paris and Ostend to Copenhagen when the service was restored in 1947.

In its heyday, Ostend was the starting point for numerous night trains heading to Central and Eastern Europe, allowing connections to be made from England via ferry services from Dover. In 1972, for example, the daily Ost-West Express conveyed a USSR sleeping car from Ostend on the two-night journey to Moscow. There was a daily sleeper to Vienna in the Ostend-Wien Express, as well as sleepers to Milan, Bern, Brig and, in the winter sports season, to Chur in Switzerland. The Tauern Express conveyed a daily sleeper from Ostend to Salzburg and on Winter Fridays a sleeper left Ostend for Bolzano in northern Italy. Over the years, Ostend gradually lost all its sleeper services.

To coincide with the opening of the Lille–Brussels high-speed line and the introduction of Thalys services between Paris and Cologne in 1997, the Nord Express was cut back to start from Cologne. Passengers from Paris, Brussels and Ostend now needed to travel by day train to connect with the sleepers, complicating what was previously a straightforward through journey. Two years later, in a decision that seemed to betray a complete lack of historical awareness, the iconic name Nord Express – one of Europe's great trains for over a century – was dropped in favour of Hans Christian Andersen. The fact that the famous Danish author of fairy tales was already in his grave long before the Nord Express carried its very first passengers seems to add insult to injury. However, the ephemeral nature of our times meant that Hans Christian himself soon fell by the wayside, to be replaced by the name Borealis when the train became an Amsterdam–Copenhagen service. The through sleepers to Copenhagen eventually ceased to operate altogether and passengers had to change at Hamburg.

If you look up Paris in the index of the European Rail Timetable today, Copenhagen is not even listed as a destination. A journey between these two capitals now requires at least two changes of train. Nevertheless, there is still a way of making the journey overnight, although the route is very different from that of the old Nord Express. Today's dedicated night traveller starts by taking an evening train from the Gare de l'Est in Paris to Mannheim in Germany. There, just before midnight, a nightjet sleeper train run by Austrian Railways leaves for Hamburg, where a connection to Copenhagen is available. The nightjet starts from Zurich in Switzerland and goes nowhere near Austria, but in 2016 Austrian Railways bravely stepped in to take over the international City Night Line sleeper services formerly operated by German Railways, which were due to close. Unfortunately, the journey does not work so well in the southbound direction unless the traveller is prepared to leave the sleeper at Mannheim at 04.40.

When I used the Nord Express in 1986, the train left Ostend before six in the evening, with the overnight journey taking more than fifteen hours. Sadly, I did not enjoy an uninterrupted night's sleep, first because I had rather overindulged at lunchtime in the restaurant of the *Prins Albert*, a fine ship of the Belgian Marine, and secondly because passengers boarding in Germany seemed intent on spending as much time as possible carousing and later sampling the duty-free goods they had just bought on the train ferry between Germany and Denmark. This was the Night Ferry experience all over again! Undaunted, I was up in good time to take in the Danish landscape as the train sped north from Rødby Ferry to Copenhagen in the early light of a frosty morning, the sunrise lighting up the morning mist and autumn colours.

Bottenviken

From Copenhagen I made the forty-five-minute crossing by Jetfoil to Malmö in Sweden and began my journey to the far north by travelling on the scenic coastal route to Göteborg (Gothenburg). There I caught a train called Bottenviken (Gulf of Bothnia), which was

Right: A 1927 art deco poster for the Nord Express by A. M. Cassandre. Russia was off-limits after the 1917 Bolshevik Revolution, so the poster shows the train's new eastern destinations of Riga and Varsovie (Warsaw). (Author's collection)

Below: Ostend station – the departure point of the Nord Express for Copenhagen. (Author, 1985)

A colourful mix of vehicles on the Nord Express as it travels through Denmark near the end of its journey to Copenhagen. Behind the loco are Danish day coaches, followed by German Railways coaches, then the blue sleepers partly hidden by the trees, and finally Belgian railway vehicles. (Horst Ebert, 1995)

Nord Express sleepers after arrival at Copenhagen. (Author, 1990)

conveying the sleeping car to Luleå that was to be my resting place for the night. It is easy to forget just how vast Scandinavia is. For example, the distance by rail from Gothenburg to Narvik, the journey I was about to make, is 1,873 km – almost as far as London to Rome.

Railways came late to sparsely populated Sweden and Norway, with many main lines not being built until the twentieth century. It was decided early on that trunk routes should be owned and run by the state. Most overnight trains were thus operated by the national railway, the Wagons-Lits company only gaining a foothold after the Second World War with some international services to Stockholm. Probably the most ambitious of these was the Italia Express, which included a through sleeper from Rome to Stockholm, taking two nights to complete the 1,740-mile journey.

In 1982 Swedish Railways (SJ) had around 200 sleeping cars, which had been built between 1946 and 1965. Unlike most European sleeper compartments, whose doors open outwards into the corridor, risking injury to anyone who might be passing at that moment, Swedish sleeper compartments have sliding doors. Snug inside a traditional warm wood-panelled compartment with the train making steady progress and relatively few stops, this time I enjoyed a better night's rest – mercifully without train ferries, duty-free shops or noisy passengers. I woke to find the train ploughing northwards through a white landscape. After sunrise came hundreds of miles of forests and lakes, the sun low in the sky, its constant flickering between the trees dazzling the eye as the train headed north. Everywhere was frozen solid. It was almost midday when I finally reached Boden, although the train itself still had further to go before journey's end in Luleå. The long-standing name Bottenviken was changed to Lapplandspilen (Lapland Arrow) in 1989, but that name ceased to be used in 1992. Because of the great distances involved, night trains continue to play an important role in Sweden and a train still runs nightly from Gothenburg to Luleå, complete with sleepers and a restaurant car, although it is now routed via Stockholm.

Into the Arctic

At Boden I changed to the train that would take me across the Arctic Circle to the city of Kiruna. The trees became noticeably more spindly and reindeer foraged near the lineside. Sunset was at 2.20 p.m. and, by the time Kiruna was reached, shortly before four, darkness had fallen. There was thick snow everywhere and the temperature was −8°C. The next morning I had time to look round Kiruna, Sweden's most northerly city, in the daylight. Since the end of the nineteenth century, the hills outside the town have been mined for their vast deposits of iron ore. The town was founded in 1900, shortly before the completion of the railway, which continues to be used to transport the ore in massive trainloads, principally across the border to the ice-free Norwegian port of Narvik. Sweden maintained its neutrality during the Second World War, but Norway was invaded by Germany in 1940, and the availability of Swedish iron ore from Kiruna was of major importance to the German war machine. Mining activity is gradually eroding the hills, some of which now resemble gigantic stepped pyramids, and is undermining the city itself to such an extent that it is in the process of being moved and rebuilt several kilometres away.

In putting an itinerary together for a journey such as this, it is sometimes easy to miss the obvious. The journey from Kiruna to Narvik was scheduled to take less than three hours, but because of the sparse train service, there was no other combination of trains that would allow me to travel the whole route in daylight. I was bothered by this apparently inefficient use of time – there would not be much travelling, but probably too much free time in the cities at each end. What never occurred to me was to wonder why it took almost three hours for the train to travel just 168 km. I was about to find out.

The train from Kiruna to Narvik had a name: Nordpilen (North Arrow). Some of it, including a sleeping car, had come from Stockholm overnight, reaching Kiruna at 11.10 a.m. Here the sleeper and the other Stockholm coaches were dropped off, with just a portion from Luleå carrying on to Narvik. Being November, there were few passengers, and I settled into an empty compartment. I expected a repeat of the endless forests of the previous day, but trees soon gave way to bare mountains and dark lakes. The depth of snow on the ground thickened as the line climbed. Spectacular views opened up as the train threaded its way between mountains and across deep gorges; now following the contours, now clinging to ledges hewn out of sheer rock faces. White and grey were the dominant colours of the landscape, but always tinged with blue, and twilight never seemed far away.

The first great landmark was Torneträsk, a long narrow lake of vast proportions surrounded by mountains, which the line skirted for miles. Then came Vassijaure, a remote settlement near a lake of the same name. Leaning out of the window to take a photograph while the train paused at the station, I was met with the profound silence and stillness that often comes with a thick covering of snow. Riksgränsen, a settlement near the border, was next, followed by Bjørnfjell. Across the border in Norway, Bjørnfjell is so remote that in 1986 it was still awaiting completion of its first proper main road to Narvik. This was the most spectacular part of the journey as the line negotiated the mountainous terrain in a series of long curves in order to gain or lose height, finally emerging high above Rombaken, the fjord leading down to Narvik. Halfway along, Rombaken is bridged between two spits of land by the road to Tromsø and Norway's far north. The railway is high enough to give a bird's eye view of this fine piece of engineering.

Narvik's setting is superb, being surrounded by mountains and fjords. The city itself is rather less beautiful, dominated as it is by a huge dump containing the iron ore brought by rail from Kiruna. So here, amid the vast, beautiful wilderness of northern Norway, is an unpretentious working town earning its living in a very practical way. To celebrate my arrival at this ultimate railway destination, I checked into the Grand Royal Hotel and enjoyed a steak dinner with wine from the opposite end of Europe. The bill for dinner, bed and breakfast was eye-watering. If I had thought Sweden expensive, then Norway was in a class of its own.

Nordpilen

The next day it was time to begin retracing my steps and head for home – a journey that would take me three days and two nights of almost continuous travelling. My train was the return working of the one I had used the day before: Nordpilen. So the portion from

Most remaining sleeper services operating in Germany are now provided by Austrian Railways' nightjet services. A double-deck sleeping car is seen here at Zurich on a service to Hamburg. (Kevin Biétry, 2017)

The Nord Express and other through sleepers had to be shunted onto a ferry to reach Copenhagen. Here, sleeping car No. 3905 on a through working from Italy – possibly the Italia Express from Rome to Stockholm – is loaded on to the Danish ferry *Sjælland* following the restoration of services after the end of the Second World War. (Collection JJB, 1950)

It's almost midday and the sleeper from Gothenburg to Luleå has reached Boden, near journey's end. (Author, 1986)

Arctic powerhouse – Kiruna. (James Losey [CC BY-NC-SA 2.0] via Wikimedia Commons, 2013*)

Narvik consisted of day coaches for Luleå in Sweden, while the overnight coaches for Stockholm were attached at Kiruna. In the meantime, it was sufficiently light to marvel once again at the views from the train as it climbed out of Narvik alongside Rombaken Fjord and, at around two o'clock, watch the setting sun striking the snowy tops of the surrounding mountains as darkness began to envelop the landscape.

At Kiruna, I needed to change carriages and find my compartment in the newly attached sleeping car. With its varnished wood interior and plush seating, it seemed older than the one that had brought me north a few days earlier; in fact, I was astonished to find that it was the same age as myself, dating from 1949. It was already dark when the train left Kiruna, but it would be many hours before the seats in my compartment needed to be converted into a bed. In the meantime, I had brought plenty of reading material from the office to while away the long hours, and there was a hot meal to be had in the restaurant car: meatballs and a baked potato in silver foil. Most meals I ever had on Swedish trains seemed to consist of much the same. The journey from Kiruna to Stockholm took seventeen and a half hours, so at 10.15 the next morning I arrived well rested, well fed and well read. The name Nordpilen disappeared around the year 2000, but the train still runs nightly and the Stockholm–Kiruna sleepers now go right through to Narvik.

My reserved seat in the train to Copenhagen was located in a kind of double compartment or saloon, where the two rows of three-a-side seating were separated by two armchairs and an occasional table, giving a very spacious and relaxing feel, with plenty of legroom and space for luggage. As always on Swedish trains, a coat rack with hangers was provided, along with newspapers neatly arranged on the table, a carafe of drinking water and paper cups – all very civilized. In comparison with my marathon overnight journey, this was a comparatively short run – just eight and a half hours – time enough to admire the Swedish landscape, have lunch in the diner and then watch the slick operation as the through carriages were shunted on and off the train ferry between Helsingborg (Sweden) and Helsingør (Denmark).

After dinner in Copenhagen, I boarded car No. 131 of the Nord Express for the sleeper journey to Cologne. Early the next morning, I emerged from the train to be greeted by a watery sunrise over the mighty Hohenzollern Bridge, which carries the railway across the Rhine. The station platform also affords one of the best views of the gigantic Gothic confection that is Cologne Cathedral. I had plenty of time to grab a sausagey breakfast at a stall in the station underpass and to observe the comings and goings of the morning rush hour.

I had all day to reach Ostend so, rather than take the usual route straight across Belgium, I made a detour through the Netherlands and arrived at Ostend two hours before sailing time. There in the platform stood the coaches of the Nord Express, including the sleeper for Copenhagen on which I had set out on my journey to the Arctic almost a week before. Tempting as it was to do the whole trip over again, I boarded the ship for the four-hour crossing to Dover and from the deck watched the train slip out of the station en route for Scandinavia. One final pleasure awaited – dinner in the ship's small silver service restaurant, which rounded off this amazing trip and put me in a mellow mood to face the rigours of British Rail's Southern Region on a Friday night.

Iron ore train at Vassijaure in a snowstorm. (David Gubler: Own work [CC BY-SA 3.0] via Wikimedia Commons, 2009*)

The railway from Kiruna to Narvik runs through spectacular landscapes. This view of Rombaken Fjord was taken from the train. (Lyonel Perabo, 2014)

Narvik from the air.
(Benutzer:Jojo86 [CC BY-SA 3.0] via
Wikimedia Commons, 2005*)

Narvik station. (Author, 1986)

Old-style Swedish sleeping car No. 4639, built in 1958, is now located at the Swedish railway
museum at Gävle. (Luis Rentero Corral, 2015)

A Swedish sleeper compartment in day mode. (Author, 1986)

A sleeping car corridor. The wooden compartment doors slide rather than open outwards. (Author, 1981)

Cologne at dusk. The railway crosses the Rhine on the Hohenzollern Bridge before curving into the station situated near Cologne Cathedral. Many of my southbound journeys on the Nord Express ended here. (Carsten Rehman, 2018)

To Finland

First, Catch Your Sleeper

I made two trips to Finland in 1991 and 1992, both of which entailed travelling continuously for two days and nights on the way out, and the same on the way home. The plan for the 1991 trip included a scenic journey along the Rhine to Frankfurt, a sleeper to Copenhagen, a night sailing across the Baltic and two days travelling in Finland before returning to Sweden 'over the top' of the Gulf of Bothnia, finishing with two nights in sleepers from northern Sweden to Ostend. It all needed a prodigious amount of planning and arranging, but everything almost fell apart when the first day nearly turned into a disaster.

It was a bit windy in the Channel, but the Jetfoil from Dover set off with not much more than a slight swell to contend with. The journey seemed to go well but as the scheduled arrival time in Ostend approached, it became clear that the Jetfoil was going to be late. I was due to connect into a through train to Cologne, but as the Jetfoil approached its berth adjacent to the station, I had a perfect view of my connection pulling out on time – and I was not on it. The magnitude of the situation did not strike me at first. I knew the next Cologne train was two hours later but, as I had allowed myself over three hours to catch my sleeper in Frankfurt, I was not too worried.

Only when I scrutinised Cook's European Timetable in more detail did the full horror of my predicament become apparent: the next train to Cologne had no connection to Frankfurt on Saturdays. My arrival there would not leave me the three hours I had planned to make the connection, nor one hour as I had assumed, but just seven minutes. Seven minutes to get off the train, leave the platform, find the right platform for my sleeper, find my carriage and get on board – in one of the largest stations in Europe – and all this only if arrival in Frankfurt was on time. I have had some nail-biting journeys on these trips, but the next ten hours were some of the longest and most uncomfortable I ever experienced.

Not for the first time, I began to question my sanity. Why on earth had I decided to travel to Frankfurt to catch a night sleeper to Copenhagen when the Nord Express offered the same facility from Ostend, the very place where I was now marooned? The answer to that was quite straightforward – a day spent travelling across Belgium followed by an early

The Jetfoil terminal and railway station at Ostend. (Author, 1993)

A vintage Trans Europe Express set near St Goarshausen, on the Rhine. The views were not so good after dark on my 1991 journey! (Christoph Schneider, 2017)

dinner in the restaurant car taking in views of the most spectacular sections of the Rhine knocked spots off spending long hours waiting for the Ostend–Copenhagen to depart. It is useless to deny, however, that there were several occasions during the course of the day when I sincerely wished that I had chosen that simple, boring solution.

I decided the best plan was to make as much progress towards Frankfurt as quickly as possible, rather than minimising the number of times I needed to change. There was, I reasoned, some chance of finding earlier connections than appeared possible from Cook's so that my ultimate nightmare of having only a few minutes to make my crucial connection might just be avoided. So I caught the next train to Liège rather than waiting for the through train to Cologne, but this achieved nothing and I ended up on the through train anyway. By 18.37 I was at Cologne, by now somewhat hungry, having only been able to manage a sandwich and a cup of tea while my head had been buried virtually non-stop thumbing through Cook's to see if I could find any quicker way of reaching Frankfurt. A half-hour wait, this time for a train to Mainz, gave me the opportunity to grab a snack; gone now any prospect of obtaining, let alone enjoying, a meal in the dining car gliding along the banks of the Rhine, by now in total darkness.

Mainz was reached at 21.03. I had just over the hour to reach Frankfurt, but, maddeningly, there was no earlier connection than the 21.38 departure, which turned out to be running late – just a few minutes late, but those minutes were now all that stood between me and my sleeper. I urged the train on; it seemed sluggish. Arrival time in Frankfurt was scheduled for 22.09, but by then the train was still cantering through the suburbs. At 22.14, the Intercity at last pulled into the platform at Frankfurt, suddenly bathed in the lights of the station under the vast overall roof. I had just two minutes left to catch the sleeper and was standing by the carriage door, ready to make a run for it and looking for any sign of its whereabouts. Then, miracle of miracles, I realised that the carriages on the adjacent platform were labelled up for Copenhagen and, as my train at last came to a stand, saw that my sleeping car was there, directly opposite me across the platform.

I heaved open the door of the Intercity and, with all my strength, drained by ten hours of jangling nerves anticipating the fatefulness of this moment, ran directly across the platform, scattering passengers in my wake and knocking sideways a litter bin in my path. The door to the sleeper was closed but not locked. I flung it open, threw my bags on board and myself after them, taking the sleeping car conductor by surprise. He had evidently thought his job of greeting passengers boarding at Frankfurt already done. Quickly realising that this quivering wreck who had so rudely interrupted the peace and quiet of car No. 197 was in fact one of his passengers, he took charge of my bags and led me to my empty compartment and berth No. 41 towards the centre of the coach, by which time the train was already on the move. I had made it! Against all the odds I was back on track! Elated, I ordered the best he could offer by way of a celebratory meal – a bowl of soup and a half-bottle of Sekt – and enjoyed them in the comfort of my cabin on a train I thought I would never catch.

This particular sleeper had started its journey in Basle, Switzerland, and was a new addition to the timetable in 1991. For many years there had been a sleeper from Frankfurt to Copenhagen, departing in the afternoon, but major improvements to line speeds enabled it to start back from Basle, allowing a much later departure from Frankfurt. Once City

This platform was the only part of Frankfurt station I saw when I caught my sleeper to Copenhagen by the skin of my teeth. (Pascal Poggi, 2015)

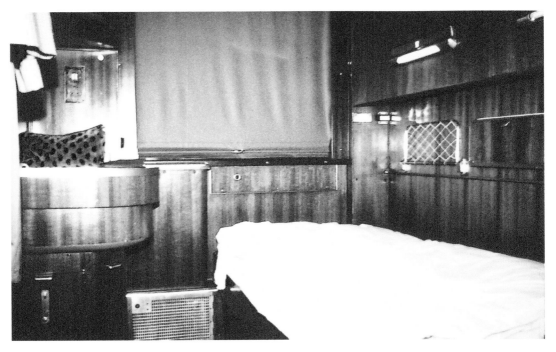

The interior of a sleeper compartment, with the bed made up. The upper berth is folded away and on the left is the covered washstand. (Author, 1988)

A sleeper from Germany, seen on arrival at Copenhagen. (Author, 1991)

This sleeper from Stockholm has arrived at Malmö station with a slightly battered door. (Luis Rentero Corral, 2015)

Night Line took over the service, the train was named Aurora. It was discontinued in 2014, when CNL withdrew all services to Denmark and France, but an Austrian Railways nightjet train still provides a sleeper service between Zurich, Basle and Hamburg, from where passengers can connect into a day train for Copenhagen.

An Easier Way

After this near disaster, in 1992 I resolved to take the easy option when I made my second trip to Finland. This time I played safe and joined the Nord Express at Liège for the journey to Copenhagen. I received a prompt and attentive welcome from the sleeping car conductor and reflected that there was still a touch of romance about travelling by sleeper. Although it was now twelve years since I first encountered one of these T2-type sleepers, which had been built in the 1970s, they still had a modern feel and gave a smooth and comfortable ride. It was still mid-evening so I relaxed and read for a while in my compartment until the conductor came to make up the bed. Everything was as it should be – the crisp white bed linen, the upper berth folded away, the lidded washstand with heavy porcelain chamber pot like some giant gravy boat concealed beneath, the mirror-fronted cupboard for toiletries, and the coat hangers with rubber studs to muffle the sound as the motion of the train swung them gently against the compartment wall. Only a party of noisy passengers boarding at one o'clock in the morning temporarily disturbed the peace until Danish passport control brought the sleeper to life again at 06.30. The attendant delivered my breakfast tray as the train sped north through southern Denmark, the trees a riot of autumn colour, mist hanging over the fields, wind turbines on the hilltops and spectacular bridges linking the islands over stretches of water several kilometres across.

At Copenhagen I took a taxi to the Jetfoil terminal in a mad dash along empty roads at this early hour on a Sunday morning. The Jetfoil was then a principal link across the Øresund, the stretch of water separating Denmark from Sweden, Copenhagen from Malmö, before construction of The Bridge. There was plenty of activity – several freighters, including a Russian rust-bucket, and some small fishing vessels. The sky was overcast but an occasional burst of sunlight glinted on the water. Eventually Malmö loomed out of an orange glow on the horizon, with the outline of a massive crane dwarfing nearby blocks of flats. An immensely tall factory chimney pumped smoke into the atmosphere as if it were the source of the entire leaden sky.

From Malmö an express took me north at the start of a 1,700-km journey to northern Sweden through birch and conifer woods. The line crossed empty roads, their surfaces shining in the rain, seemingly miles from any human habitation apart from isolated wooden farmhouses in various pastel colours with their gables and corners picked out in white. At one o'clock I went in search of lunch in the light and airy restaurant car, whose welcoming staff spoke English with an ease that put my own language skills to shame. I chose a fillet of pork with creamed mushrooms. The meat was as tough as old boots, but tasty. The restaurant was doing excellent business, but I felt a bit dowdy in comparison with many of my fellow passengers, who looked as if they had just stepped out of a clothes catalogue featuring brightly coloured woollens.

At Mjölby I changed from my Stockholm-bound train to one heading for Gävle, where I was to pick up my next sleeper. The lineside birch trees resembled cascades of yellow snowflakes. Unruffled by any breeze, the lakes – including Vättern, one of Sweden's two vast inland lakes – were deathly calm. As dusk began to fall, the train's mournful monotone whistle and the warbling of the carriage lights played a continuous duet. Outside, lamps shone out from the windows of farmhouses and other wayside signs of habitation.

Round the Gulf of Bothnia

Having kept perfect time all day, the train stopped for fifteen minutes in the middle of nowhere to allow a late-running train to pass in the opposite direction on this single-line section. This was worrying as my next connection was tight, so the rest of the journey became another nail-biting one. At Gävle, to my great relief, my train to the north was waiting, and I joined my somewhat ancient but cosy sleeping car on board Nordpilen. The snow outside was much thicker by the time I turned in, but I was snug in my compartment and spent a peaceful night with scarcely a sound to wake me, and no noisy passengers like the night before.

In the morning, the snow cover reflected what little light there was as the train thundered through seemingly endless pine forests. In clearings, smoke rose vertically from house chimneys in the still morning air. Lakes and rivers were frozen. The birches here had lost all their leaves and every twig was covered with thick frost. By eight o'clock the sun was up, highlighting the browns and greens of the pines against a clear blue sky. At Älvsbyn I discovered that Nordpilen was running well over an hour late. According to the conductor, the previous train had a wheel-flat, and because the outside temperature was –20°C, the track had to be inspected in case of a broken rail. He added that the scheduled bus connection to Haparanda would probably have left, so a taxi might have to be provided instead. Meanwhile, the train had stopped in a tunnel, the inside of which was like an ice cavern.

By the time the train reached Boden, the sky had clouded over and it was snowing gently. Here, Nordpilen was divided into sections – one for Luleå on the coast and the other for Kiruna, inside the Arctic Circle. The train was roughly an hour and a half late and the bus for Haparanda had indeed departed. As quite a few of us wanted to make the connection, Swedish Railways managed to conjure up – heaven knows how in this far northern outpost – a stretch limo to take seven of us on the 165-km journey. With very little other traffic, and with snow continuing to fall, our limo cruised in stately fashion down the centre of the forested road, the journey accompanied throughout by a Roy Orbison singalong tape played at full volume. By Haparanda, road conditions were becoming difficult, but the driver willingly took two of us on to Tornio across the frozen river that marks the Finnish border.

In 1991, when I travelled this route in the opposite direction, I found myself with an enforced wait of nearly an hour and a half at Haparanda. At that time there was still a train service to Boden, but by the following year it had been discontinued and replaced by a bus service – or, in our case, a stretch limo. Haparanda station turned out to be an architectural gem,

Right: The washstand and mirror-fronted cupboard in a Swedish sleeper compartment. The wooden finishes give the compartment a cosy feel, especially when there's thick snow outside. (Author, 1992)

Below: Lapplandspilen, the overnight train from Luleå to Malmö, is seen at Boden, in northern Sweden. (Edwin Walton, 1976)

Haparanda station, where European standard gauge meets Finnish broad gauge. (Author, 1991)

The waiting room at Haparanda. Did Lenin wait here? (Author, 1991)

which also had a claim to a small place in history. It was a great barn of a building in brick and timber; built in 1917, it was all gables and verandas and steeply sloping roofs. It was intended to be a major international transit point where passengers changed from the Western European gauge of Swedish Railways to the broad gauge of Russian Railways, Finland then being under the rule of imperial Russia. Its passenger facilities were split between two levels linked by an ornate staircase with timber balustrade. The waiting room was wood-panelled, with pictures of Sweden set into the panels over the seats and travel posters displayed above. There was elaborate tiling everywhere, and furniture with exquisitely carved detailing.

Soon after it opened, Haparanda station was called on briefly to play host to one of the most transformative figures of the twentieth century as he passed through on his way to Russia. Together with some associates, Vladimir Ilyich Lenin had been permitted by the German authorities to travel in a sealed railway carriage from Switzerland, where he was in exile, in the hope and expectation that he would foment the revolutionary forces that were in play in Russia and undermine the Russian war effort. The First World War meant that fighting between Germany and Russia had closed all other ways of reaching Russia by land, so the new railway border crossing at Haparanda was the only route available. There, Lenin transferred to a Russian train for the final leg of his journey to St Petersburg, where he would go on to lead the Bolshevik Revolution. A plaque at Haparanda commemorates his brief visit.

After the stretch limo had dropped me in Tornio, and with Roy Orbison still ringing in my ears, I caught a bus to Kemi railway station. Having dumped my bags in a huge locker, I sought out the one place I really wanted to see on this journey – the northern edge of the Gulf of Bothnia. It was an awe-inspiring sight, with the sea completely frozen as far as the eye could see. The snow crunching satisfyingly underfoot, I returned to the station for my train to Oulu. The sun set in a blaze of colour and the branches of the pine trees drooped under their heavy coating of snow.

Despite Oulu's attractions, I found myself spending time at the railway station, a timber building of quite some size with a homely interior hermetically sealed from the intense cold outside. But as always, it was the trains that caught the attention – especially the procession of three sleeper trains heading for Helsinki, the last of which had started in Rovaniemi and also conveyed sleepers for Turku. A similar pattern of services continues to operate today, but two of the trains have been extended northwards to start from Kemijärvi and Kolari inside the Arctic Circle. I would very much have liked to try one of Finland's sleepers but I was put off by the warning in Thomas Cook's publication *European Sleeping Cars* that single occupancy of a sleeper compartment in Finland requires the purchase of two first-class rail fares and two sleeper supplements. That seemed like an extravagance too far.

My 1992 visit to Finland ended at the port city of Turku, where I had some time to look round Finland's oldest city – and its former capital under Swedish rule until 1809. In Swedish, Turku is known as Åbo, and there remains a Swedish-speaking population along Finland's coast. Having retrieved my cases, I took a taxi to the Siljatama, from where my ship to Sweden was to depart. Although the cabbie spoke no English, I was driven to the harbour accompanied by Elgar's 'Pomp and Circumstance March No. 1' blaring out of the car radio, the final stages of the ride being to the strains of 'Land of Hope and Glory'. Altogether, it had been quite a musical trip.

Night Boat to Sweden

The *Siljatama* was a seething mass of people, with long queues at the ticket office and check-in. At around 7.30 p.m., there was an undignified surge as the boarding gate was opened and everyone shoved on board. After an excellent dinner in the restaurant I slept well, but woke briefly in the early hours to find the ship rolling about somewhat alarmingly. Awake at six for a seven o'clock arrival, I decided there was time for breakfast before disembarking. At 7.20, while taking my time in the restaurant, there was an announcement in English for the occupant of cabin No. 6209. That's me! I gulped down the last piece of roll and the rest of my coffee and made for the desk – whatever was the matter? 'We need to clean your cabin. The ship leaves again for Finland at eight'. What I had failed to notice was that the people who were having breakfast when I arrived were, like me, travelling from Finland to Sweden, but those now in the restaurant had just boarded to make the journey in the opposite direction. Panic! I returned to my cabin most apologetic. I had left my belongings strewn all over the place and there was nothing for it but to throw everything into my suitcase and disembark at once. The by now underemployed customs officers eyed me suspiciously as, somewhat dishevelled, I shambled sheepishly past their post, the last passenger off the ship.

Stockholm was in the middle of a snowstorm. I first noticed this while having breakfast and assumed it was fog as the TV tower was barely visible. The train from Central station made a prompt start but progress was slow and it quickly became clear that it was going to be badly delayed. Despite this, no information was provided to passengers for over an hour and a half, proving that British Rail was not unique in being unable to cope with heavy snow or in failing to keep passengers informed. Trees were bent double under the weight of snow and in a few cases large branches had snapped off, and this turned out to be the cause of the delay. The train was worked wrong line past blockages caused by tree branches falling on to the overhead wires. Abandoning my original plan to explore some secondary routes in southern Sweden, I diverted to Gothenburg and found to my relief that the Oslo–Copenhagen train was running on time. It delivered me to the Danish capital in good time to catch my final sleeper – the beloved Nord Express.

Going Home

The night train was at the platform early. I was surprised to see the Betten Frei sign illuminated on car No. 131, the Copenhagen–Ostend sleeper, indicating that there was space available for any passengers wanting to upgrade at the last minute. In over a decade of using it, my experience was that it was nearly always full. The pleasant young conductor told me that it was unusually quiet with only eight passengers booked. Unfortunately two of them were in the compartment next to mine and, yes, they were intent on buying their

The frozen sea on the northern shore of the Gulf of Bothnia, Kemi, Finland. (Tapani Launonen, 2013)

Oulu station. (Author, 1991)

A sleeper, bound for Helsinki, waits at Oulu. (Author, 1991)

Wellamo, a Silja Line ferry, which ran from Turku to Stockholm. (Franz Airiman, 1988)

duty-free at midnight on the ferry, returning around 00.30, chattering away about the goodies they had bought and slamming the compartment door. Peace was finally restored around one o'clock.

I left the Nord Express at Cologne and made a short tour of the tangle of railways in the Ruhr district, ending up in Aachen on the Belgian border, from where I caught a train to Ostend. After Brussels it was a pleasant afternoon as the train sped through the flat fields of Flanders with its prosperous towns and neat villages of tall thin houses, small fields no larger than a garden, broad canals, tall regimented poplars in dead straight lines, and severely pollarded willows. Near Brugge, a herd of cows waited patiently in line in anticipation of milking time. Now the train turned towards the glowing orange sun for the last time, past the barn bearing the faded lettering 'Ostende' alongside the painting of a boat, the rest of the message too faint to pick out except for 'vers l'Angleterre'. At Oudenburg, where the line rises above a canal, the first warehouses of Ostend came into view. Then, still at speed, the train passed marshalling yards full of passenger carriages, including some ancient Wagons-Lits, their blue paint faded and the windows long gone, before finally gliding into Ostend station precisely on time.

The harbour was busy. A dredger made a dreadful din as it went about its work, bringing buckets full of silt slurping upwards from the depths. Once the barge alongside it was filled with muck, it left to dump its load at sea. Two pleasure craft came in, a trawler departed and various coasters were waiting to enter. The *Reine Astrid* sailed at 5 p.m. As she broke harbour, the setting sun was reflected in the windows of the seafront buildings that stretch away into the distance; a thousand panes glinting red as the ship moved out to sea. Suddenly the sun disappeared behind a bank of cloud and the sea glowed milky red. It was getting cold so I went inside, anxious now to find the restaurant for the last dinner of my trip. After some difficulty, I eventually discovered a tiny restaurant hidden in the stern of the ship – just four tables, white linen and one waiter. I was asked to share a table already occupied. It was a delight: a good menu and wine list, sixteen places with fifteen diners – not bad for such an elusive establishment. An aperitif, three courses, a half bottle of St Emilion, coffee, chocolates and port all made for a delicious finale to the trip, with a continuous view of the lights of the Belgian and French coasts drifting by.

I have to confess that my enjoyment of this gastronomic treat was tinged with sadness. In an increasingly self-service world, this excellent little restaurant – banished to an obscure corner of the ship because so few passengers wanted what it had to offer – seemed to be on life support. Although I did not know it then, so were many of the sleepers that took me to the farthest parts of Western Europe in the 1980s and '90s. High-speed rail was revolutionising train travel and the opening of the Channel Tunnel in 1994 proved to be a game changer. Eventually it became possible to make the journey back to England from places such as Milan, Berlin and Barcelona in a single day without having to use night trains. I did not give up on sleepers altogether, but instead of having to rely on them to get me to and from far-flung places, I found myself using them once I got there; for example, to travel from Galicia to Zaragoza in Spain, or to cross Poland. For me, it is a cause of regret that the European sleeper network is a shadow of what it was, but progress is impossible without change and this sometimes means the loss of something special and precious.

Sleeper train at Stockholm Central. (Pete Hackney, 2009)

A sleeper for Paris is seen on the Nord Express before its departure from Copenhagen. (Author, 1995)

Ferries at Ostend under a threatening sky. (Author, 1993)

Ostend at sunset. (Wolfgang Staudt, 2009)

Gone but not forgotten: this destination plate from a carriage of the Orient Express features an impressive list of calling points. Constantinople became Istanbul after the foundation of modern Turkey in the 1920s. The journey from Paris to Istanbul took three nights, and the last through sleeper ran in 1977. (Pablo Martinez Perez, 2013)

Acknowledgements

I would like to thank the following people for permission to use their photographs in this book: Alisdair Anderson, Andrew Bone, Bert Kaufmann, Carsten Rehman, Christoph Schneider, Cornelius Koelewijn, Dominique Desmares, Fabio Miotto, Franz Airiman, Horst Ebert, Jesús M. Velasco, John Law, Jorge Almuni Ruiz, Kevin Biétry, Luis Ignacio Alonso, Luis Rentero Corral, Lyonel Perabo, Michel Ledieu, Miguel López Galán, Milica Vujicic and Edwin Walton., Pablo Martinez Perez, Paolo Taesi, Pascal Poggi, Pete Hackney, Robert Carroll, Roger Sutcliffe, Tapani Launonen, Torrego family and Wolfgang Staudt. I have used some images under the terms of Creative Commons licences. These are denoted by an asterisk.